BUNNY MELLON
Style

BUNNY MELLON
Style

LINDA JANE HOLDEN,
THOMAS LLOYD,
AND BRYAN HUFFMAN

FOREWORD BY TORY BURCH

GIBBS SMITH
TO ENRICH AND INSPIRE HUMANKIND

First Edition
25 24 23 22 21   5 4 3 2 1

Published by
Gibbs Smith
P.O. Box 667
Layton, Utah 84041

1.800.835.4993 orders
www.gibbs-smith.com

Designed by Rita Sowins / Sowins Design
Printed and bound in China

Gibbs Smith books are printed on either recycled, 100% post-consumer waste,
FSC-certified papers or on paper produced from sustainable PEFC-certified forest/controlled wood
source. Learn more at www.pefc.org.

Library of Congress Control Number: 2021931006
ISBN: 9781423654926

Cape Cod
1968
Bun's hat

Remembering Bunny,
with love and admiration for her
unerring eye and enduring style

CONTENTS

FOREWORD

BY TORY BURCH

ONE OF MY FAMILY FRIENDS HAD A HOUSE NEAR THE MELLON PROPERTY ON ANTIGUA, and on our way home to New York from a family holiday in the Caribbean, my mother, my sons Henry, Nick, and Sawyer and I visited King's Leap. I knew it would interest my mother, who is an avid gardener, as, of course, Mrs. Mellon famously was—my mother has been organic gardening at our farm in Pennsylvania since the early 1970s.

As soon as I arrived at King's Leap, I was struck by its immense beauty and felt an immediate calm. I exhaled. I relaxed. I was filled with a sense of serenity. It almost felt like I had been there before. I knew I wanted to return, many, many times more.

The way the house was planned by Mrs. Mellon with the architect H. Page Cross as a series of pavilions is a masterpiece. Every access has a point of view and is intentional. There is nothing frivolous, just beauty, balance and integrity. It's like heaven on earth. Every room is the essence of restraint and has a purpose. When I told my husband, Pierre-Yves Roussel, that I thought we should acquire the property, we talked it over and agreed it was a project we could do well together. We bought King's Leap.

Since the property had been unoccupied for over ten years, as you might imagine, it needed to be revived a bit. I asked the architect-interior designer Daniel Romualdez to help me with the house, and I knew Miranda Brooks would be perfect for the gardens. We found information and inspiration from photographs, from descriptions of the house in Paul Mellon's autobiography, and also an extensive memo that Alison Harwood, a *Vogue* contributor, wrote in the 1960s to Diana Vreeland. She told Mrs. Vreeland that King's Leap "played at unpretentiousness, pretending to be as casual as the blue-denim wrap-around skirt and floppy-brimmed cloche devised for Mrs. Mellon's working costume by Mainbocher," one of her favorite dress designers.

How do you improve on perfection? You don't. You do what needs to be done and try to make sure that afterwards you really can't tell what the interventions were. I tried to honor Mrs. Mellon but also put my own spin on the place. We are a different family dynamic. For one thing, I turned a boathouse into a bunkroom where all the boys, there are six, hang out. I think that's one of the main reasons why the house works so well for us.

The longer we know King's Leap, the more situated I feel, and Mrs. Mellon is like a teacher. Some of the people who helped the Mellons are still here and I love to hear their stories. When lemons fell from the trees, Mrs. Mellon told them to leave them exactly where they fell, don't pick them up, they looked great, natural. She asked her decorators to make the interiors look like "some things were brought down from the attic."

Restraint brings attention to the integrity of design, just as it does to any creative expression, whether it's how you decorate, entertain or how you dress. With a symmetry to everything she did, Mrs. Mellon's perfectly imperfect approach to her houses, and to her gardens, is a triumph of restraint.

Some of the people who work here or visit us tell us that they feel Mrs. Mellon's enlightened presence. Miranda felt it when she was reviving and expanding the gardens. My mother says that Mrs. Mellon came to her room one night to visit. I was stunned when I found a painting here by the Louisiana folk artist Clementine Hunter, who painted the first piece of art that I ever bought.

Mrs. Mellon has had a massive influence on every person in the design and garden world that I know. Even just the way she found colors, drawing from the natural world, or from fabrics, painting a floor the color of denim or sand. Everyone copies her, everyone references her, including me.

Her voice was subtle and restrained but her influence will be everlasting. "Nothing should be noticed" was her motto. As with Linda Jane Holden's earlier book, *The Gardens of Bunny Mellon*, I am thrilled that this book tells the story of this extraordinary woman, her talents, unerring eye and wonderful spirit.

PREFACE

BY LINDA JANE HOLDEN

DURING THE LAST DECADE OF HER LIFE, Bunny Mellon often said that God was her "friend," and declared the ongoing events in her life had been the result of "happenstance." Webster's dictionary defines happenstance as "a circumstance especially, that is due to chance." *The Oxford Advanced Learner's Dictionary* defines the word as a "blend of happen and circumstance," and "chance, especially when it results in something good." The research process and writing of *Bunny Mellon Style* has been an exceptionally rich journey that, despite the hurdles and obstacles across our path, did lead to "something good." As we veered together down one rabbit trail after another, we always seemed to end up on Bunny's path of chance, where good things had happened—and were happening again. Happenstance!

In our quest to understand the influences of Bunny's "style," we reached out into the world at large, and as we did, we began to realize how large a life she had led. It's all there. One just has to look for it.

Thomas Lloyd and I participated in the White House Historical Association's 2019 symposium "White House Gardens," where we met Cindy Sidey Buck, daughter of renowned journalist Hugh Sidey. Cindy introduced me to *Mona Lisa in Camelot*, which is a marvel of a book by Margaret Leslie Davis, and *Dinner in Camelot* by Joseph A. Esposito, which describes in great detail the guests who dined with the Kennedys when they hosted forty-nine Nobel Prize winners, along with other scientists, artists, and writers.

Bunny's father, Gerard Lambert, step-mother Grace Lambert, and maternal grandfather, Arthur Houghton Lowe, committed many words to the page. Lambert's autobiography, *All Out of Step*, provided a wealth of material, as did his second wife Grace Lambert's biography, *A Life of Grace*, as well as the charming exchange of letters between Arthur Lowe and his young granddaughter, many of which she preserved. Lambert wrote in exacting detail about his building projects, making it clear that, like father like daughter, "nothing was ever done. There was always more to do." Due to his amateur status as an architect Lambert leaned heavily on the skill set of the American country house architect Harrie Lindeberg, who had been influenced by the famed British architect E. L. Lutyens. Lutyens, in turn, was inspired as a child by the charming and imaginative scenes in the children's literature of Randolph Caldecott. The historical societies of Princeton, New Jersey, Rindge, New Hampshire, and Fitchburg, Massachusetts, and the Preservation Foundation of Palm Beach, Florida, filled in the gaps, providing glimpses into the past, as we unraveled a few mysteries. *Carter Hall and the Civil War*, by Stuart E. Brown, Jr., and Ann Barton Brown, and a personally guided tour of the estate by John and Mary Walsh of Project Hope, lent flavor.

Bunny's self-published library catalogs, *Sylva*, *Flora*, *Pomona*, and *Herbaria*, served as excellent resources. Billy Baldwin, Bunny's longtime friend, wrote of his experiences with Bunny in several beloved books that profile his design acumen.

John Baskett coauthored Paul Mellon's *Reflections in a Silver Spoon* and curated the Mellons' collection of English and French Impressionist artwork for over twenty years, up until the time of Paul Mellon's death in 1999. Baskett, who made yearly visits to the Mellon homes in Washington, D.C., Upperville and Cape Cod, shared interesting and informative stories from his storehouse of memories. The Mellons' son-in-law, Derry Moore, the 12th Earl of Drogheda and a world-class photographer, also graciously shared his insightful thoughts and impressions and reminisced about Bunny's style. Also writing from the UK were Lambert family friends Nancy Astor and her niece Nancy Lancaster, both Virginia transplants, who documented their relationship with the Lambert family in letters and books. Mitchell Owens has filled a vault with voluminous material, including his interview with the designer Imogene Taylor, who worked with John Fowler, of Colefax and Fowler, bringing his vision to Bunny in America.

The Lambert Foundation published a catalog titled *Drawn to Beauty: The Art and Atelier of Jean Schlumberger*, filled with lavish photography, for an exhibition of the Schlumberger jewels held in the Museum of Fine Arts, St. Petersburg, Florida, from December 15, 2018–March 10, 2019. And Hubert de Givenchy curated an exhibition at the Cristóbal Balenciaga Museoa from May 27, 2017–January 25, 2018, with an accompanying catalog titled *Rachel L. Mellon Collection* that featured her couture.

Hubert de Givenchy and Philippe Venet hosted me (Linda) for lunch (yes, it was an amazing experience!) at their home on Rue de Grenelle in Paris in the fall of 2015 to discuss gardening with Mrs. Mellon. Givenchy and Bunny Mellon had worked together to restore Louis XIV's vegetable garden, le Potager du Roi, at Versailles, and Philippe had been at their sides. At the time of our luncheon, Givenchy was organizing a gardening exhibition in the north of France. Both gentlemen expressed regret and dismay that the maquette that Bunny had commissioned for the study and restoration of the garden, and donated to the Palace of Versailles, had disappeared. As they continued their joint commiseration at lunch over the seeming failure to locate the maquette, I lifted my hand as if to ask permission to speak. I remember they both turned their heads and looked at me as I told them "I know where it is," with timid excitement. "You couldn't possibly," they answered, somewhat apologetically as they shook their heads from side to side. So, I pressed on and described the maquette in full detail and they finally believed me!

It was luck. The day prior, my cousin Rodney Robinson, a prominent Wilmington, Delaware, landscape architect, and I had visited the vegetable garden where the director, Antoine Jacobsohn, had taken us on an extensive tour. Louis XIV had revered his gardener, Jean Baptist de La Quintinie, who had made the garden for him and built a house adjacent to the garden for himself and his family. It was on the second floor of this house that Rodney and I first saw Bunny Mellon's maquette and photographed it.

GIVENCHY GENTLY INSTRUCTED THAT AFTER LUNCH WE WOULD SIT TOGETHER IN THE SALON, he would show me his garden scrapbooks, and then I would show him my photographs of the maquette. Within the hour, preparations had begun to transfer the maquette to Givenchy's exhibition.

During the years of their friendship, Bunny corresponded at length with Givenchy, faxing handwritten missives ornamented with her whimsical drawings. In this case, modern technology was on our side—the fax machine. Bunny kept the originals after they had been faxed. Givenchy passed away in the spring of 2017 (before finishing his introduction for *The Gardens of Bunny Mellon*).

In the fall of 2019, Bryan and I went to Paris to visit with Philippe Venet, armed with a handwritten note from Thomas. I don't know what the note said, but it brought a smile to Philippe's face as he read it. After reminiscing with him, Bryan and I stepped into the garden planted with white roses. Upon reentering Givenchy's salon, we were surprised to be met by Doris Brynner, preeminent member of the international jet-set, fellow patron of Schlumberger and Balenciaga, and the "mastermind" behind Dior Home, who provided fun and enlightening background information on the threesome and put us in touch with famed landscape architect Madison Cox.

Cox had known Mrs. Mellon and M. Givenchy and shared stories with me about his first visit to Oak Spring, when he thought he had the wrong address. Madison also shared with me how he had to make certain there were ripe apples hanging on a lone apple tree high above the city known as the Big Apple on a certain day when two certain people would be having tea. That's just a bit of his greatness! Artist and gardener Abbie Zabar provided precious insight into the experience of shopping with Bunny in New York City, filling gift baskets with her signature products.

Thanks to Meryl Gordon, I was fortunate to interview Samantha Leonard, daughter of artist Paul Leonard, who inherited a bevy of materials that document her father's work for Bunny Mellon. Susan Leopold—Bunny's former librarian and who assisted Bunny in the creation of her third catalog, *Herbaria*—provided keen insight into the research process at Bunny's library, which was akin to an adventure on the high seas of learning.

I am grateful to Okey Turner for the details he provided on the design and construction of the Memory House. Appreciation goes to Lisa Rockwell, Draza Stamenich, and Jay MacMullan for their research assistance. I am grateful to Christopher Spitzmiller for sharing his memories of Bunny, and to Brooke Shealy Myatt and Matt Kramer for gaining access to the wealth of photos at the Virginia Museum of Fine Arts and Sotheby's. Thanks to Igor Uria Zubizarreta, Director of Collections at the Cristóbal Balenciaga Museum, for his kindness, patience, and sharing photography from the museum's fine collection.

Anne Slater Coyner, Gray Coyner, and George Thompson led me on several driving expeditions up and down the back roads and around and across the surrounding landscape of Upperville, Virginia, in pursuit of their Piedmont Hunt, being ever so careful not to break the fox's scent and pointing out along the way the farms the Mellons had purchased from her grandmother, Tacie Slater. Anne's parents, Kitty and George Slater of West View Farm in Upperville, had been friends and neighbors of the Mellons and fox-hunted with Paul Mellon.

Loving thanks and appreciation go to Marie Colandrea, whom Bunny titled her handmaiden because she provided a friendly hand when Mrs. Mellon's eyesight was diminishing. They discussed the details and daily routines of running the houses and enjoyed reading through *Mrs. Beeton's Book of Household Management* together. Additionally, butler John Baltimore and housekeeper Maria (pronounced Mariah) Dorsey from Oak Spring and Linda Evora, who worked as a housekeeper at the Cape Cod house, gave insight into Bunny's management style. Lisa Rockwell, who successfully gardened at the Cape with Mrs. Mellon for over twenty-five years, shared secrets of Bunny's gardening techniques as well as her innovative storage ideas, creating stow-aways out of stair treads, hiding book shelving in empty wall spaces, and adapting an eighteenth-century American colonial for life in the twenty-first century.

On Nantucket Island, photographer Daniel Sutherland provided beautiful images that appear in the book and shared insight with Bryan and me into the construction of the Nantucket house, which he helped to build. Also on Nantucket, Liz Winship, Bess Clarke, Rebecca Peraner, and the weavers at Nantucket Looms shared the stories of Bunny's collaborations with Andy Oates, founder of the Looms.

Sotheby's series of catalogs from the Bunny Mellon auction held in the fall of 2014 provided detailed information and answered many questions we wished we could have asked Bunny. The efficient and expert work of staff assistant Maryrose Grossman at The John F. Kennedy Presidential Library made it possible to bring the story to life.

We owe a debt of gratitude to Tory Burch and her husband, Pierre-Yves Roussel, for their welcoming spirit and for sharing their home in Antigua with us—the house that was built by Bunny and aptly described by Tory in the foreword. Their poignant recollections on the King's Leap restoration and the joy it has brought to their family are so appreciated. They continue the house's tradition of making a place so unique and special for children and guests alike.

It has been a wonderful adventure exploring Bunny Mellon, how her style developed and played out in her homes and what she wore, and to realize the impact of her taste on the world. No matter where we go, people always want to know more about Mrs. Mellon. Her influence endures!

MEMORIES *of* GRANBUNNY

I BEGAN THE EXPLORATION OF MY GRANDMOTHER'S LIFE BY ASKING MYSELF A SIMPLE QUESTION: Is it possible to improve a relationship with my grandmother after her death?

My earliest memories of Granbunny, as I called her, were as a timid little boy observing her from a distance. I would see her working in her beautiful gardens in Cape Cod, pruning her beloved apple trees while wearing that blue hat and skirt. I came to understand that she was a creative force in everything she did, be it flowers, art, pruning or design work, and I longed to know her better. Even as an adult I had no idea how to forge a more intimate connection with her. But that dynamic changed in the last eight years of her life with the births of my two children, Teddy and Fiona, her great-grandchildren. Their collective fearlessness, which I certainly lacked as a child, brought joy and laughter to my grandmother as she embraced their energy.

The children would run into her living room in Oak Spring, shouting her name and eating Lay's potato chips out of a white plastic cylindrical container she kept them in. She would always sit in her corner spot on the sofa and top off her Clamato Bloody Mary with that secret little bottle of Stoli. My daughter took her first steps in that room, and they weren't to me but to Granbunny. Sometimes, the children would run up to her bedroom to greet her and would knock over an enormous collection of treasured mementos she always surrounded herself with. It was then that I discovered my grandmother was a pack rat. I grew to appreciate this tendency in her, and it provided even greater insight into who she was as a person. She saved a vast collection of letters, drawings, postcards and other forms of correspondence as part of her Oak Spring Garden Library collection; it was a seemingly infinite personal timeline of her amazing life outlined through thousands of ink strokes carefully laid to her signature Granbunny-blue stationery.

It was this initial dive I took individually into her writings that began the spark for initiating discussions about this book concept with Bryan Huffman, my dear friend and a friend of my grandmother, and Linda Jane Holden, author of *The Gardens of Bunny Mellon*. Linda's various discussions about her own book underscored the question so many people had about my grandmother: Who was she really? Through the past year, I've had the distinct pleasure of learning more about my grandmother and what led her to become the public persona so few people actually knew.

The collective but distinctly different roles that her father, Gerard B. Lambert, and grandfather Arthur Lowe played in establishing her love for the natural world, gardening design, and space planning laid the groundwork for understanding her formative personality. In their own ways, both men fostered the self-confidence that would ignite her creative genius and unquestionable work ethic. Arthur Lowe was a supporter of her whimsical childhood visions of fairy tales and animals—something that developed in her own style with gardens and jewelry.

Gerard Lambert introduced her as a child to the Olmsted brothers' team, unearthing a resource from which she squeezed every ounce of information for her first garden project at Albemarle, her father's house in New Jersey.

I came to understand how Granbunny's early gardening experiences enabled her to master-mind greater projects in years to come, such as her house and garden at Oak Spring in Virginia. The two important men in her young life, who she loved dearly, gave her the platform to develop garden skills and self-assurance that ensured her success as a women in a male-dominated world. Realizing this was a good starting point for me.

Granbunny's consistent drive for creative perfection—explored through the prism of colors, animals, and space design—paired well with her uncanny ability to seek out and partner with some of the greatest emerging designers of the time, specifically Jean Schlumberger and Hubert de Givenchy. They developed wonderfully symbiotic friendships and together created some of the most iconic personal clothing and jewelry collections of the twentieth century.

The greatest discovery about Granbunny's character came, however, through insights of the various people who surrounded her daily. The most poignant aspect of her personality was her generous nature toward others. She exhibited unquestioned loyalty and support to so many people around her—most notably her loyal employee base, which at one point in time had an average annual tenure of over twenty years. Although this kind of personal employ was foreign to me—and, indeed, to most anyone else—it became her most endearing trait as I began to interview and talk with so many people who worked for or knew her for many years.

She also shared this generosity with the many guests and dear friends she hosted through the years at her various properties around the world. Granbunny created spaces that were not only beautiful but that appealed uniquely to each of her guests. She never looked for credit; simply the joy of knowing that these wonderful spaces brought her guests true happiness was all she needed. Now, looking back at my time spent at her houses and the amazing memories they left me, I realize this was her gift to me—and for Granbunny, I now realize, the greatest sign of love she could show someone.

I have a greater appreciation for Granbunny because of the process of co-creating this book, and delving into her life and legacy is a journey that I will continue. My hope is that every reader experiences a bit of the joy and special feeling she gave to those of us who were lucky enough to feel it firsthand.

I miss you, Granbunny.

INTRODUCTION

THERE WAS A TIME WHEN THE PORTRAIT OF A GREAT LADY, a masterpiece known as the *Mona Lisa*, sailed the Atlantic on a journey to America, where it was placed on exhibition at the National Gallery of Art in Washington, D.C. The news of her arrival was announced over the airwaves and splashed across newspaper headlines. "She is here!" Leonardo de Vinci's masterpiece was "the most important single work of art ever to cross the ocean," heralded John Walker, then director of the National Gallery of Art. Indeed, she did arrive on American shores "with all the care due a lady of her high station and fragile beauty," observed Margaret Leslie Davis in *Mona Lisa in Camelot*.

It was January 1963. To celebrate the upcoming exhibition, President John F. Kennedy and his wife, Jacqueline, presided over a celebratory dinner at the French Embassy "worthy of da Vinci himself," boasted Davis. The dinner menu "began with a delicate foie gras followed by *filet de boeuf Charolais sous la cendre garni renaissance*," a hearts of lettuce salad with mimosa dressing, and a finish of "poached pears, swaddled in hot chocolate sauce, bundled into a pastry shell," and "trailed by a superb Dom Pérignon 1955."

At this dinner was Jackie Kennedy's quiet and unassuming mentor and friend, Bunny Mellon, and her second husband, Paul Mellon, a trustee of the National Gallery of Art. The Mellons were enjoying the moment, happy to help yet insisting, especially in light of the mysterious, last-minute, $50-million gift that financed the exhibition, that "the Mellon name should not appear anywhere."

"I was in America in 1963 and remember the unveiling of the *Mona Lisa* at the National Gallery of Art. It caused quite a stir," John Baskett, curator for the Mellon Art Collection, told me during one of our discussions. "As you know, Carter Brown [who at the time was an assistant to John Walker, the director of the National Gallery of Art] was enthusiastic in promoting blockbuster activities." Baskett added, "In the case of the Mona Lisa, I was given to understand (not by Paul Mellon) that Charles de Gaulle allowed the loan as a political gesture, having just refused Great Britain access to the European Common Market and wishing not to offend the United States, who was a close ally of Britain." Most important, Baskett added, "the French were not given to lending such national treasures, and there wasn't any other reason to make the loan at that time. Paul would have been consulted, but he always tried to avoid involvement in politics."

The National Gallery of Art had been a gift to the nation by Paul Mellon's father, Andrew Mellon, a Pittsburgh banking and business tycoon and three-time Secretary to the U.S. Treasury. Even today, the gallery's permanent storehouse includes the art collections of Andrew Mellon and his two children, Ailsa Mellon Bruce and Paul Mellon, and Paul's wife Bunny.

LEFT: Mrs. Kennedy is pictured with Nicole Alphand, wife of the French Ambassador to the United States Hervé Alphand; photo detail. **RIGHT:** First Lady and art enthusiast Jacqueline Kennedy, adorned in a strapless pink silk chiffon evening gown embroidered with porcelain beads and rhinestones, dazzled her guests at the unveiling of the *Mona Lisa* at the National Gallery of Art. It was said that *Mona Lisa* was matched only by the enigmatic beauty of the First Lady herself; photo detail. (Both photos: Abbie Rowe. White House Photographs. John F. Kennedy Presidential Library and Museum, Boston.)

A LIFE OF HAPPENSTANCE

For Bunny Mellon, life was a balancing act. Married to Paul Mellon, she played the role of "wife of"—when in reality, as she told Bryan Huffman during one of their first conversations, she had wanted to be a stage designer. "After I graduated from Foxcroft, I wanted to go to school to study stage design. But my father [Gerard Lambert] forbade it." Instead, Lambert insisted her job was to get married and produce children, and he handed her a list of eligible bachelors from whom to choose. From this list she chose first husband Stacy B. Lloyd of Philadelphia, with whom she produced two children, Stacy III and Eliza.

To compensate for feeling stunted by the lack of a higher education, Bunny took to viewing her circumstances as opportunities to set a stage. Parties, dinners, exhibitions, and events held at the National Gallery of Art or at one of the Mellons' far-flung estates were transformed into magically creative experiences. Citing one such occasion, former art dealer Franck Giraud told the *Financial Times* in "A Cultivated Taste: The Bunny Mellon Auction," that the Mellons "gave a big dinner at the National Gallery, and she asked for [her] Rothkos to be hung around the room." For the same dinner, Bunny designed the table settings, which featured the sculpture of artist and friend Betty Parsons. Bunny is remembered for making the rounds to specifically thank each person who had worked with her on these events.

For decades, carefully selected masterpieces from Bunny and Paul's collections were placed on public display, a striking contrast to the closely guarded atmosphere of their private lives. For Paul Mellon, the idea of garnering power and prestige and having his name in the papers held no appeal whatsoever, he revealed in his autobiography, *Reflections in a Silver Spoon*, cowritten with John Baskett. What did appeal to him was the idea of privacy. In her book *Grace and Power: The Private World of the Kennedy White House*, Sally Bedell Smith compared the Mellons to Edith Wharton's characters the van der Luydens, who "stood above all of them" and "faded into a super-terrestrial twilight." Smith, who personally knew the Mellons, described them as "shy and gentle, the ultimate in discernment, seldom seen on the party circuit." Marion Oatsie Leiter, a former D.C. socialite, told Smith that for the Mellons, "everyone had to come to them." But, not until an invitation had been issued, whether it was a formally engraved summons or a playful drawing describing an upcoming tea party.

The American decorator Billy Baldwin was surprised to receive an invitation to the coming-out party of Bunny's daughter, Eliza Lloyd, in Virginia on June 16, 1961, and a second invitation a few weeks later. "Of course I went to Virginia," he said in his autobiography, *Billy Baldwin: An Autobiography*, written with Michael Gardine. Remembering his first visit to Oak Spring, which is located in the Virginia hunt country, Baldwin wrote:

ABOVE LEFT: Bunny with I. M. Pei doing what she does best: using her "eye" to set a stage in the East Wing of the National Gallery of Art. **MIDDLE AND BELOW LEFT:** This dinner was in honor of *The Splendor of Dresden: Five Centuries of Art Collecting, an Exhibition from the German Democratic Republic*, 1978. The trapezoidal shape of the East Wing building lot was Bunny's inspiration for having the dinner tables created in the shape of trapezoids. This posed some interesting decorating challenges, including how to use tablecloths. She solved the problem by wrapping the tables with cloth and attaching them underneath so there would be no uneven overhanging of the fabric. Her herb topiaries softened the angularity of the scene. **RIGHT:** The stage is set for guests under the giant Calder mobile in the tower; photo detail. (National Gallery of Art, Washington, DC, Gallery Archives. 26B, National Gallery of Art Event Images. Photograph by Jim Sugar. 26B4_22284_006.)

Bunny and Paul greet the gratin of Washington society at a National Gallery dinner; photo details. In the photo middle right is J. Carter Brown, then-director of the National Gallery; all details. (National Gallery of Art, Washington, DC, Gallery Archives. 26B, National Gallery of Art Event Images. TL & TR, 26B4_304_021, 26B_304_023; ML & MR, 26B4_304_026, 26B4_304_027; BL & BR, 26B4_304_024, 26B4_304_033.) **FACING ABOVE AND BELOW LEFT:** For the preview dinner of Impressionist and Postimpressionist paintings from the USSR, April 1973, Bunny created magnificent arrangements incorporating "fake" flowers with real ones to create eye-popping colors. Note the flowers have Bunny's airy touch and

are set in her favorite containers, woven wicker baskets; details. (National Gallery of Art, Washington, DC, Gallery Archives. 26B, National Gallery of Art Event Images. Above, 26B4_304_005; below left, 26B4_304_002.)
FACING BELOW RIGHT: Mr. And Mrs Mellon with Mr. and Mrs. I. M. Pei at the inaugural dinner in the newly opened East Wing celebrating *Splendors of Dresden: Five Centuries of Collecting from the German Democratic Republic,* June–September 1978. Bunny wears a Givenchy dress sashed at the waist with a blue ribbon; detail. (National Gallery of Art, Washington, DC, Gallery Archives. 26B, National Gallery of Art Event Images. Photograph by Jim Sugar. 26B4_456_001.)

You can't imagine how wonderful it feels to be in that house and in those greenhouses. You know that she loves every chair, you know that she feels tenderly about every single blossom, and you know that she rips out anything that she doesn't like, not with violence or cruelty, but with the simple determination to eliminate it. Hers is a regime of no tolerance for the mediocre.

The Mellons conducted this private, privileged life at their four-thousand-acre farm in Virginia and at various other houses and apartments in Paris, New York City, Cape Cod, Nantucket, Washington, D.C., and Antigua, their island paradise in the West Indies. They preferred to go quietly about their lives together, in the worlds of philanthropy and art, and separately—he in horse breeding and racing and she in books, gardens, and design.

The famed British photographer Derry Moore, the 12th Earl of Drogheda and Bunny's son-in-law married to her daughter, Eliza Lloyd, commented that the Mellons' houses "always surprised, which is incredibly rare." He wrote me, "What I think was most remarkable about Bunny's houses was their individuality. The Antigua house was quite different to Oak Spring, as was the Cape Cod house, which was also totally different to Antigua." As far as colors, he added that the Cape Cod house was done in "blues and whites," and the palette for Antigua was warm, with "oranges, browns, and greens. New York was different, too, although I'm not sure how I would characterize it. I recall yellows and blues." Derry pointed out that Bunny "was absolutely sure of her vision and the things that influenced her were absorbed—digested one might say— rather than simply attached." Of course, not to be overlooked, Derry said, "It was very fortunate that she had limitless funds and extraordinary taste, two things that almost never go together. I would also say that among her faults, vulgarity was totally absent."

While Bunny acknowledged that her tastes were simple, she wrote in a journal that "the quality is expensive—and I'm extravagant." She felt "it is wasteful to be mediocre. There is no middle line between simplicity and the best. . . . If you know the best [then you can] if you have to, live beautifully with very, very little."

Bunny was self-taught, what she described as "learning by oneself," in the areas of interest dear to her heart and the ones she pursued: art, couture, horticulture, interior design. She wrote in her journals that being "motivated by our own will and curiosity to learn has many advantages. You do not have to follow a road laid out for you, nor are you intimidated by rules that kill an original thought before it is born. You can take your time allowing for time to be sidetracked, which will add an unexpected dimension." Experience taught Bunny that "there is nothing that has not already been done in design. It is the joy of discovery that creates the excitement, and interest of putting together old ideas with the originality of the individual person."

CREATIVE INFLUENCERS

Bunny's early years were shaped significantly by two important men: her father, Gerard B. Lambert, and grandfather, Arthur Houghton Lowe—two successful businessmen with strong ideas of their own, both of whom taught her to savor the things around her. Her journal notes read, "It is hard to find someone who you can have a conversation with—ancient values of right and wrong. It is as if it all disappeared with my father and grandfather—where their advice and guidance could be counted upon. Today it is rare."

As she moved through life, Bunny developed strong collaborative relationships with a few other creative experts: of course, her second husband, philanthropist and horse enthusiast Paul Mellon; the jeweler Jean Schlumberger; two preeminent couturiers of the twentieth century, Cristóbal Balenciaga and Hubert de Givenchy; decorators Syrie Maugham, Nancy Lancaster, John Fowler, Billy Baldwin and Paul Leonard; architect H. Page Cross; and garden landscape architect Perry Wheeler and gardener Irvin Williams. She sought out artisans such as Andy Oates, creator of Nantucket Looms, and New York iron monger Paul Fiebiger, whose collaboration with Bunny lasted well over fifty years.

Her imagination and creative expression expanded in the world of art. While Bunny's taste in artwork favored the French Impressionist paintings of note that she collected, she also chose the strikingly bold and modern works of Mark Rothko and Diego Giacometti, while fostering emerging talents such as Madeline Hewes, Sophie Grandval and Mossy Fuller. Her spirit of creativity and originality was always sparked when collaborating with these visionary artists.

ABOVE: To celebrate the opening dinner for the National Gallery of Art's first exhibition of modern art in 1973, Bunny loaned several of her Mark Rothko canvases to adorn the walls. For the table décor, she persuaded Betty Parsons to loan her brightly painted wooden sculptures to serve as the centerpieces. When J. Carter Brown took over as director of the National Gallery, he initiated the practice of having dinners in the museum itself. He leaned heavily on Bunny to facilitate many of these evenings.

THE EARLY
YEARS

FATHER'S INFLUENCE,
Gerard B. Lambert

THE AXIOM "MORE IS CAUGHT THAN TAUGHT" CERTAINLY WAS TRUE OF BUNNY MELLON as she grew up in her father's orbit, his "way of life—of living"—in Southampton, where she had spent many summers as a child and "sang in the choir of the Dune Church," and at Albemarle, the family's 400-acre estate in Princeton, New Jersey, where she was surrounded by "beautiful things" and an enjoyment of people, family and music.

Despite her engaging environment, "We never really talked," she wrote in an essay about Gerard B. Lambert titled "My Father." By her own admission, Bunny's education had been "haphazard; a year of Shakespeare plays, or English literature—nothing that would make a formal college." Instead, she felt that her education had almost been a consequence of living in her father's shadow and observing him in action. Lambert did things in a big way, which she found fascinating, and to store all of this valuable information she made what she described as a "great vault" in her mind and filled it with things "to think about, mostly in terms of shapes, colors and feelings."

According to his daughter, Gerard Lambert never discussed his philosophy of life or living, but, she said, "he gave me one." From him she learned the importance of setting goals and working hard to achieve them, and to keep moving forward. Lambert was a brilliant businessman who enlarged his family's inherited Listerine fortune by repositioning the product and expanding its market base through sheer wit and a can-do attitude. He never "talked about business unless in the sense of a game like chess—a challenge or a fascination." He set goals, and when a goal had been reached, he moved on. Lambert was a soft touch for anyone he considered disadvantaged and he gave money freely. When he gave it, "he just gave it" and didn't "expect anything in return." However, most of Bunny's feelings about her father were "observations." She said that they "never discussed life or anything to do with it."

Gerard Lambert was orphaned at a young age along with his four brothers and a sister; they spent childhood summers in Albemarle County in the Blue Ridge Mountains of Virginia. Neighboring Mirador was a lovely colonnaded house, home to the famous Langhorne sisters, two of whom later traded America for England while still clinging fiercely to their beloved Virginia roots: Lady Nancy Langhorne Astor, of Clivedon—the first woman elected to the House of Commons—and Elizabeth Langhorne Perkins, whose daughter, Nancy Perkins Lancaster, was the widely recognized creator of the elegant British country-house style and former owner of the interior design firm Colefax and Fowler. Lambert, like the Langhorne sisters, cherished the faded elegance of Virginia's aging plantation houses and the gardens of their youth, where the aromas of boxwood and magnolia gently wafted over a pleasant tangle of decay that remained from the war-torn South of their time.

Bunny's mother, Rachel Lowe Lambert, "was always in her room" because "she hated the sun," or so the children were told.

Bunny set sail with the significant men in her young life—her maternal grandfather, Arthur H. Lowe, and her father, Gerard B. Lambert—along with her mother, Rachel Lowe Lambert.

There were three children: Rachel "Bunny," the eldest, was born in 1910; Gerard Jr., nicknamed "Sonny," followed in 1912, and Lily in 1914. Gerard Lambert wrote in his autobiography, *All Out of Step*, "There is something primitive in us that makes us feel differently about a son who bears our name. We do not feel quite the same about any other child." And of daughter Lily, Lambert's second wife, Grace Lambert, was quoted in her biography, *A Life of Grace*, by George Pitcher: "She was his baby, and he adored her." Consequently, "being a child not often noticed" by her family at Albemarle, Bunny felt "freer than either Lily or Gerard to live in it." And live in it she did—she watched, and learned, and gradually over time developed a sharp eye for design.

ALBEMARLE, BUNNY'S CHILDHOOD HOME

Albemarle, named for the county in Virginia, was a three-story, thirty-two-room mansion constructed of a rough and uneven kiln-warped brick that was whitewashed and then weathered to give the feeling of timelessness. Gradually, the house became what Gerard Lambert described as "a thing of great beauty." Grace Lambert later remembered that building Albemarle "almost ruined him financially and turned his hair prematurely gray from worry."

The house project began in 1913 when Lambert, who "had a passion for collecting houses," wrote Grace, assembled a four-hundred-acre tract in Princeton, New Jersey, and went to work

"at once" with Harrie Lindeberg, "the American Lutyens," an accomplished architect with the firm McKim, Mead & White, the same firm that President Teddy Roosevelt commissioned to remodel and renovate the White House.

The surrounding landscape was "designed and planted" by the Olmsted Brothers of Boston, and a "tall Dutchman . . . was in charge," Bunny wrote in her journal. "Every day after school I watched and looked at plans in a shed up by the greenhouse."

To the east, a high wall was built and became, wrote Bunny, "the beginning of the big garden; from it was cut a wide allée to a stony brook—here the vegetable garden was made from what had been a corn field—a long lilac walk with flowers and low-growing plants. Along the walk to the tennis court were tiny flowers—all whose names I remembered and plants I have since used."

The garden wasn't done in a hurry, but "grew as gardens should," and before she knew it, Bunny had learned "how to plant and about plants." Bunny wrote that it was this knowledge, this practical, hands-on learning experience of watching the tall Dutchman and studying the plans every day that helped her years later to design gardens for family and friends—even those living at the White House. After the Rose Garden was completed in 1962, "a controversy arose" when a landscape company called into question the legitimacy of the garden design. The garden had received enormous publicity—"Surely an amateur could not have done it alone. . . . There must have been a ghost designer." At first, she couldn't take the accusation seriously. It seemed incredulous. But then, Perry Wheeler, a local landscape architect who, along with Irvin Williams, had worked with her on the garden, asked Bunny if she would agree to meet with Mr. Zach, past president of the American Society of Landscape Architects. They met in the Rose Garden.

Mr. Zach was "a nice man," who had expected a sort of "pompous blue-haired garden club woman who did not really plant on her hands and knees," she wrote.

> *We talked, it was very easy. He asked where I studied and I said "never." . . . I had just lived in my father's house and had learned by the things that happened there. I explained that the garden had been designed by Olmsted in Boston and I tagged along to listen. [Zach] smiled and said: "I was an apprentice on that job. I learned from the same plans when I was a very young man." He knew the Dutchman and he knew the plans. The Landscape Association of America has never questioned me again.*

Just as Bunny Mellon had been inspired by the artwork of Beatrix Potter, Kate Greenaway, and Henriette Willebeek Le Mair, the architect Harrie Lindeberg had been inspired by E. L. Lutyens, whose architectural pedigree was rooted in the picturesque drawings of Randolph Caldecott featured in children's books of the era, i.e., *The House That Jack Built*, and for whom

ABOVE AND BELOW: The formal gardens at Albemarle, the Lambert family home in Princeton, New Jersey, where Bunny had her first garden, a fifteen-by-fifteen-foot plot sited near the dining room. The house was designed by Harrie T. Lindeberg. Frederick Law Olmsted, Jr., designed the gardens and grounds.

the prestigious Caldecott award is named. With ceaseless wonder, Caldecott drew charming images of country living, houses built with materials that related to the earth—half-timber façades, tall wood-shingled peaks and pitched gables, glazed windows, interiors with exposed beams and patterned floors, and front doors painted in bright colors of yellow—all of which created a charming sense of place and exuded a blissful feeling for country life, imagery that was made to order for the Lambert family home, Albemarle.

Lambert and Lindeberg took their time—two years to draw the house design and another two years to build it. The inspiration for Albemarle house was Lindeberg's Colonial Revival–style James L. Breese house in Southampton, Long Island, whose prototype had been George Washington's plantation house, Mount Vernon. Lambert and Lindeberg replicated Washington's river-facing portico, which is supported by tall, square-shaped wooden columns, but Lambert wanted Albemarle's columns to be round. Lambert documented the painstaking process; they would "put up a column and take it down, remove half an inch in diameter, and then keep on doing this until the column was right." Samples of quarried roof slate were laid out on the front lawn for study, and they "argued for weeks over a molding for a doorway." They "loved the problems and did not rush things." At odds with his strident goal-setting, Lambert believed that a project was never finished—there was always something more to do.

The entrance to the house was reached along a curved driveway lined with old, transplanted apple trees and boxwood that wound alongside a low-cut lawn of creeping bentgrass, what Lambert described as "a smooth carpet of flawless grass . . . that seemed to wrap the arriving visitor within its cool green arms." The all-green setting was tranquil, soft and cool, and Lambert was particularly delighted to hear arriving visitors comment, "What a sweet house," a refrain that brought satisfaction because it was then that he knew that his experiment in optics had been a success. Knowing that "the size of an object is determined in the mind of an observer by something with which he is very familiar," as Lambert recorded in *All Out of Step*, "and that it is these things, such as a window or a door, that give an idea of scale, you can draw the rough outline of a building and from there make it anything you like. . . . One enormous door in the front makes it a doghouse. . . . Hundreds of little windows make it . . . a factory."

Lambert's three-story main house, topped with an attic and flanked on either side with wings, was 192 feet in length yet felt "small and intimate." To achieve this

PRINCETON
NEW JERSEY

feeling, the height of the front door extended into the second floor and the windows along the front pillars were "as big as show windows." The house was built of bricks, whitewashed and allowed to weather over the years. All of this was done to make the house look old and to give a feeling of timelessness. As Daniel Sutherland, a Nantucket photographer and artistic painter who worked with Bunny until her death, told me, the Lamberts liked their houses "to look old, but not be old."

Albemarle was designed for formal entertaining, despite the fact that "Jerry wasn't very social . . . and just wanted to stay home with me," said Grace Lambert in *A Life of Grace*. There was a grand entrance hall with a floating staircase that curved upward to the second floor, and a music room for parties. For big dinners, cocktails were served in the living room or adjacent gallery, and located near the dining room was a "withdrawing room" for the ladies. Down the hall there was a library that "offered a quiet retreat for the men, with their after-dinner drinks and well-fed chatter." There were books. "Big, huge books of gardens, of architecture, of archaeology," books that Bunny took to her room to "dream over." And there were artifacts, "old dusty bottles dug up in Asia Minor."

Everything fascinated Bunny, she wrote, but there "was no one who talked to me about them," so she absorbed them into her mind to "think about."

There was another room in a corner of the house called "the office" even though it "wasn't really an office." It was in his private lair that she first came to know and appreciate her father and his way of life. The office was always locked so "no one would go in and disturb anything." However, every week at noon on Fridays and Saturdays, one of the village women, Miss Joe, would come in to clean. Miss Joe must have enjoyed being in the room, too, because she ate her lunch there and always left the door open—maybe for Bunny. These were the moments that Bunny could get inside that room to "have a look around." Bunny remembered a green carpet and that the room was filled with drawing materials: "drawing boards, paste, paints, tracing paper, T-squares, thumb tacks, and plasticine" and that "it smelt of all these things and erasures." Bunny took the "palettes, or some ink or paint or a ruler" to her bedroom, where she would use them "for a day or so" and then return them. She had no idea how to use these drawing supplies, but she "loved them and found a way." She worked at it.

In the Lambert household, on the one hand, Gerard Lambert expected perfection: brass, floors and silver were shined and polished to perfection. But on the other, chairs and curtains were allowed to become shabby and have what Bunny described as a "sat-in look," an aspect that later found its way into her successive homes.

A concurring investment in an Arkansas cotton plantation along with the building of Albemarle put a tremendous strain on Lambert's once-healthy finances. An excessive "outgo of cash"

PREVIOUS OVERLEAF: Fronted by a tapis vert, the architectural design of Albemarle was inspired by George Washington's home, Mt. Vernon, in Alexandria, Virginia.

ABOVE: The library, where Gerard Lambert entertained his gentlemen friends after dinner, and where Bunny lingered for many hours over her father's collection of fascinating and inspiring books. BELOW: Certainly, the shifting light of this parlor captured the imagination of the aesthetically inspired Bunny.

delayed the completion of Albemarle, yet he still managed to keep "the flags flying," completing the house in stages. In all the hubbub, Bunny noticed everything. She "watched furniture come in: beautiful furniture and china and curtains—curtains made of pale-yellow silk hanging from gold arrows."

At first, the children's rooms were in the attic on the third floor, where Bunny shared a room with her sister, Lily. As more rooms in the house were completed, the sisters were moved to the second floor and each had her own room. Bunny's room had big windows, a fireplace, a pretty bed and huge trees outside—design elements that would one day become part of her architectural and landscape mantra—always allowing room for improvement and working toward that elusive goal.

CARTER HALL, BUNNY'S FIRST GREENHOUSE

When Bunny chose to attend Foxcroft School in Middleburg, Virginia, Gerard Lambert was drawn back to the Old Dominion. In 1929, he purchased Carter Hall, an eighteenth-century Georgian hipped-roof mansion near Millwood, a small village in the Blue Ridge Mountains. The drive from Millwood to Upperville is fourteen minutes, and another thirteen to Middleburg by way of route 50, which is generally known as the John Mosby Highway. For Lambert, probably the most appealing aspect of owning Carter Hall was the opportunity to restore what he described as "an extraordinarily beautiful house in the Shenandoah Valley of Virginia."

The recently divorced Lambert along with his nineteen-year-old daughter, Bunny, teamed up once again with the architect Harrie T. Lindeberg and "did Carter Hall over completely." No expense was spared as the house and "household offices" were restored from the ground up. All of the buildings were insulated, roofed with clay shingles, and copper gutters and downspouts were installed. A "free flying" stairway was added and the second floor opened up. A nearby grove of oak trees received extensive tree-care, and the expansive front lawn that had been used by Stonewall Jackson and his troops was revitalized and regraded. It was here that Lambert gifted Bunny with her first greenhouse, which she designed and supervised the building of.

Just before Bunny's twenty-first birthday, her father penned a letter on August 7, 1931, and said,

> *It hasn't been hard to love you and to be proud of you. Your character, and kindness and consideration of others [have] always made me very proud to have you as my daughter. I haven't a single complaint, my baby, except that time has gone so quickly.*
> *— Your Daddy Dear*

ABOVE: Carter Hall, often called "the Hall," was completed in November 1800 by Col. Nathaniel Burwell. In November of 1862, General Stonewall Jackson staked his headquarters on the grove near the front door, where years later Bunny learned the fine art of tree care and surgery and led to the rescue of many massive oaks for years to come. **BELOW LEFT:** Rear façade. **BELOW RIGHT:** Vistas and Virginia skies marked the extensive landscape at Carter Hall.

ABOVE LEFT AND CENTER: Auxiliary buildings included a washhouse and a dairy and may have originally included a gardener's house, a shop, and shed. Wash house on left and dairy house in middle photo—precursors to Bunny's use of small auxiliary buildings found later at Oak Spring. **ABOVE RIGHT:** Bunny (left) with her brother, Sonny (Gerard B., Jr.) and sister, Lily Lambert, at a ball given for Bunny at Carter Hall. **BELOW:** Bunny's trusted butler David was so dear to her that she continued to write about him in her journals years later. Watercolor by Bee Dabney.

FACING: Even when Bunny no longer lived at Carter Hall, the historical dwelling remained in her thoughts. She was known to show up, unannounced, with works of art in hand and proceed to suggest where they should be hung. Painting by Benjamin Marshall titled *Coursing: A Gentleman with Groom and Greyhounds*, collection of Mr. and Mrs. Paul Mellon.

As Bunny was moving further into her role as mistress of Carter Hall, which included duties of managing the staff, preparing daily menus, and overseeing all household operations, David, her respected and trusted butler, assisted and guided her in navigating this new responsibility. This duty interestingly included ladling out controlled amounts of spirits, dispensed in small tin cups, to workers who often complained of "the misery" in their backs, etc.

She trusted David's instincts. To her dying day she would often quote David, remembering him fondly and his keen assessment about people as he said, " 'T ain't quality, Miss Bunny, 't ain't quality."

Carter Hall remained in Bunny's heart the rest of her life. Later owners Helen and Dr. John Walsh welcomed Bunny and her proprietary vision for the estate. Their son, John, has wonderful memories of her showing up at the front door with workers carrying large paintings from Paul's collection that she "thought would be perfect" here or there, not to mention the huge trees "she thought needed to be placed around the property, always with men and equipment to dig the enormous holes."

GRANDFATHER'S INFLUENCE, *Arthur Houghton Lowe*

THERE WERE OTHER ROOMS, houses and gardens that tangled through the strands of Bunny's memory. She spent six weeks every summer with her maternal grandparents, Rachel and Arthur Lowe, at their home in Fitchburg, Massachusetts, and their three-thousand-acre farm in West Rindge, New Hampshire, Grandpa Lowe's birthplace. "The farmhouse where he was born had burned" and he had "built a small one room cabin surrounded by a screen porch" in its place. Bunny's younger sister, Lily, wrote, "Bunny always returned home with glowing accounts of her visit and a note from grandmother saying that Bunny had been a great treasure to all of grandmother's friends." On the other hand, Lily noted, "All I could think was how glad I was I didn't have to go." Lily "loved grandfather" who was "a wonderful, gentle man with a white beard," but was "scared of my grandmother."

Arthur Lowe, an important influence in Bunny's early years, "was a very busy man" who ran several cotton mills in Massachusetts. Lowe was "a distinguished persona," wrote Gerard Lambert in *All Out of Step*, "and one of the finest men I have ever known."

Lowe directed the manufacture of gingham cloth at two mills, the Parkhill Cotton Mill and the Grant Cotton Mill; he was the president of Amoskeag Manufacturing Company of Manchester, New Hampshire, president of the Lancaster Mills in Clifton, president of the Connecticut River Power Company, vice president of the Fitchburg Savings Bank and a director of other banks in the city. He served on the state board of education and helped to develop the state college system. He served on the Fitchburg Board of Trade, was an alderman in 1888, and mayor in 1893. When Theodore Roosevelt visited Fitchburg, he stopped by the Lowes' home, where he visited with Lowe on the front porch.

"We were pals," Bunny wrote in an essay titled "My Grandfather," in 2006. In an undated letter to her, Grandpa Lowe wrote,

> *My dear Bun—How are you? Listen here! Do you know? I was perfectly delighted with your lovely fairy story—I think it is wonderful to dream and think about fairies like that. Sometimes when I dream, I see just such beautiful things. That is imagination. I am glad you have imagination. It will be splendid all your life to think out these lovely things. Do you know—when I go out in the early morning and hear the birds and the bugs and the crickets and the grasshoppers and the frogs and the flies—and see the lovely butterflies and moths and millers I wonder if they don't belong to the fairy family.*

Photographs of Bunny's beloved grandfather, textile manufacturer
and town father Arthur H. Lowe; details.

And in response to another story that she wrote, he added,

> *Your little story about being taken up into the clouds and spending the night in cloud*
> *beds in the care of angels is really beautiful. I suppose GrandMa will say that I can't go*
> *because I snore too loud. Well, I can enjoy the story just the same and last night where*
> *I saw some lovely fleecy clouds way up in the sky floating past—I wondered if you were*
> *up there sleeping in a little sky bed and had come down here to Florida to get a peep at*
> *me at Ormond.*

And then as he described the changing clouds and weather conditions, he wrote,

> *This morning they had changed into rain clouds and came down to make the flowers*
> *and fruits and berries and vegetables grow for our pleasure. Now listen here—Do you*
> *know? God makes all these lovely beautiful things and gives us the minds and hearts to*
> *know about them and to love them. He wants us to think about them and dream about*
> *them and talk about them. When we do this, we show that we appreciate the good things*
> *that he gives us.*

And there was often plain-spoken advice: "You will learn in this world that one has to do and
wants to do something for other people."

In another letter, now barely legible, Bunny wrote a poem to Grandpa, who was in Battle Creek at the time, to "remind you that you live in New England and it is as follows:"

In the woods
And mountains high
Many birds and butterflies
Flit between
The trees and sky.
In the big stone wall
Crept the little chipmunks small
    Through the mossy woods
    Runs the light foot deer
    Little flowers bud,
    And bloom,
    When their season
    Time has come

From the time she was a child, Bunny had felt a strong and abiding love for nature—plants, butterflies, birds and trees—which had been "encouraged by a wonderful grandfather who shared the same interests and was my close, dear friend." Lowe had given her a small wildflower book, *Flower Guide: Wild Flowers East of the Rockies,* that became the beginning of her own library many years later. He appeared "ageless" and was "kind" and recognized the "importance of nature as a guide to life."

Another childhood poem by Bunny Lambert:

The Bird

Nature never changes
Roses Bloom,
Trilliums fade,
And cattle creep under,
the loving shade.
And as you walk
Through the meadows green,
Little pine trees,
at your feet spring.
Thousands of little pine trees tall
swing and rock
in the breezes low
And at the top,
Of a great big hill
Sits a little house quite small
But oh, that house,
and the wooden gate,
that stands in front of it,
Is the loveliest place
On the big, round earth.

FITCHBURG HOUSE

The house in Fitchburg was a "large dark red house with a big porch on the corner" near a large park at the end of town, wrote Lily. "I can still see the big Victorian style house with a porch facing Main Street complete with rocking chairs. This porch had a view of the public gardens with a formal bandstand, and beyond that, the mills that were owned by my Grandfather and before him, his father who had left Scotland for New England."

The bandstand was surrounded by benches, and a concert was held once a week from 8:00 to 9:00 in the evening. Bunny remembered listening to the music "lying in bed in a very cozy little bedroom." The performance always closed with "The Star-Spangled Banner." She was "sent to bed at 8:30 but stayed awake until 9:00" to be a part of this "patriotic scene." She "always stood next to her bed until it finished—then bundled down to sleep." The front hall, Lily wrote, "was dark and had a great big staircase. Halfway up the stairs was what my Grandmother called a landing. On the wall was a large window with a pattern of colored glass that went from ceiling to floor. I was fascinated when the sun came through revealing the colors on the carpet."

Grandpa Lowe's library was small but cozy. Bunny remembered, "There was no door, just a dark blue velvet curtain, that you pushed aside, took its place." Often in the late afternoon or early evening after supper Bunny visited her grandpa in this library. She remembered pulling the curtain back and hearing him call to her, "Come in my child and we will read." He read to her from Alcott, Thoreau, Emerson, Longfellow and Hawthorne, "creating cherished moments" that led to her love of books and collecting them, of traveling, and of recreating scenes from the pictures she loved in her own garden designs.

LEFT: View from the park across the street from the Lowe House in Fitchburg, Massachusetts, where a band played every Friday evening. **CENTER AND RIGHT:** The Lowe House, where Bunny arrived for an extended stay every summer. President Theodore Roosevelt called on Bunny's grandfather as he was passing through town. The two men sat together on the wide veranda, and one can only imagine what they discussed.

The winters in New England were cold with heavy snow and, for convenience's sake, the outbuildings and garage "were attached one to the other" at the end of the house. In the garage, which had originally been built as a stable for horses and carriages, there was a workbench where, tended by the family chauffeur who was "king of the garage," Bunny "built boxes for flowers and a small chair for the doll house."

Just beyond the garage there was "a long garden with three terraces" that were "divided by two or three steps." On the first terrace there were "flower and rose beds"; the second was a lawn "with a playhouse on the side that had belonged" to her mother, where Bunny only went "on rainy days to sew." The lower terrace of the garden was Bunny's "most pleasureful domain." There was a "high dark green wooden wall." On the other side of the wall "there was a shop that roasted coffee and next to it a bakery." The aromas of coffee roasting and bread baking "came over the fence at different times of the day in a sort of comforting way." There were raspberry and blackberry bushes on one side and a dark green sandbox that Grandpa's carpenters had built for Bunny on the other. Nearby was a row of sweet peas growing on a "delicate wire fence." Using "a tin bucket to wet the sand and mold the designs" and "bits of twigs and old kitchen cups for ponds and pools," Bunny spent hours re-creating the gardens she "had found in gardening books in Grandpa's library." Only Grandpa and the gardeners came down to see what wonders Bunny had built.

WEEKENDS AT WEST RINDGE FARM

On the other hand, her maternal grandmother was a "strict sort of a woman in both her looks and demeanor." Bunny and her Grandpa "understood this," and "we did well keeping the peace and still had the freedom to go to Grandpa's farm," which was "always a treat." Grandpa took her to Concord to visit the homes of the great writers and Thoreau's Walden Pond. As they "took off" in Grandpa's old touring car, "it was always a great event" and they became "part of a marvelous world." There were three of them—Grandpa, the chauffeur, and Bunny. Their picnic lunch included "bread, milk, butter and root beer. Grandma's cook made blueberry and apple pies and the rest we would get up there—fresh vegetables, fruits and eggs." Their "speed was not so great and each thing we passed could be accounted for—the farm where the hay had been cut before the rain" and another "where an afternoon storm had caught the poor farmer in his efforts." The back roads were bordered with wildflowers and there was "always a new flower to see."

On Friday afternoons they "crossed the border from Massachusetts into New Hampshire" and their life "became the land." West Rindge, New Hampshire, in the 1920s, population 600, was a scene of charmed village life. "Boys played games there—and there were wooden benches for people to sit on as they were coming to and from the store," Bunny wrote.

As they entered town "there was a Grange Hall painted yellow on the right and a Basket Factory on the left. To get to the Basket Factory door you had to cross over a little stream on two wooden planks." The baskets were "predominantly made of ash wood . . . although birch and oak were also used," wrote Karla McLeod, director of the West Rindge Historical Society. She continues, "About 40 different types of baskets were made but the signature basket was a double pie basket with a woven top and removable slatted wooden tray." The baskets were "shipped all over the world for over 80 years."

Out at the farm, Bunny and Grandpa "went to sleep and woke up with the birds" and, if it was warm enough, Bunny "slept on the porch alone—watching the stars. [I] learned not to be

Archival scenes of West Rindge, New Hampshire. **LEFT:** The basket factory Bunny drew inspiration from was located near this general store. **CENTER:** Small-town America as it was in the 1920s. **RIGHT:** Property that Arthur Lowe donated to the Boy Scouts of America. It eventually became the home of Franklin Pierce University.

afraid of the animals whose eyes I would see in the dark—or Thunderstorms," which, according to Grandpa, were "God's way of telling us who is in charge." It was this love of fresh air that propelled her window and screening systems in all of her future projects, allowing for cross breezes, eschewing fake air.

Together they explored the woods and Grandpa pointed out each plant and tree "that had a story in its relation to its native surroundings." It was on her grandpa's farm "between the ages of 9–13" that Bunny "learned to understand the soil and the needs of growing things."

A child of Scottish immigrants, Lowe loved America and also instilled within Bunny a deep patriotism and desire to give back, often reminding her that America "is a great country . . . we must take care of it." When "a match company had laid waste to the adjoining forest—he bought the unwanted land and replanted it." As a farmer dug the holes, Bunny "followed with a bundle of seedling pines, dropping one in each hole. Then my Grandfather secured the earth around them." Together they planted thousands of trees and "at the end of each summer he had engraved on a boulder—how many were planted, and the year. 'For my Grandchildren and Great-grandchildren,' he smiled. The boulders are still there," she wrote. And today, it is a forest thick with pine that is almost impassable.

Bunny was the first one up in the morning and it was her job to "prime the pump and heat the water for my Grandfather's shave." There were two hand-dug wells on Arthur Lowe's land. Priming the pump was done by pouring water into the spout while at the same time lifting the handle up and down, a relatively quick but necessary process. After Bunny's chores were done, she would tidy herself up and "slip on the ribbon band that held back" her unruly hair. Then she was "free to roam the fields—or wherever, until breakfast." It was during these hours alone that Bunny began to "notice how things grew—some near a wall for protection, others in the open field. Stronger where the cows had been—spindly and fragile otherwise." She fell in love with the "joy of space—ice blue, lazy blue, dark blue, full of stars or hidden by fog. What a little world we are, looking at that sky." For Bunny, "space, and how to use it, was the beginning of every garden."

APPLE HILL WITH STACY LLOYD

IN 1932, BUNNY MARRIED STACY B. LLOYD, JR., OF PHILADELPHIA. They resided for a time on the Carter Hall estate in East House, a two-story stone house sited a few steps east of the mansion. In 1937, they purchased "next door" land and built Apple Hill, a two-story colonial-style house.

Bunny worked to integrate the architecture and landscape. This was her first true building project, one in which her intricate window screening and shutter systems were employed to maximize fresh air and cross breezes.

Sited just beyond the kitchen door were a small terrace and a greenhouse. On the terrace, four flower beds in the shape of hearts—exemplifying what she referred to as her "romantic" period—were planted with floribunda, white briar cliff, crimson glory and violets, all outlined in parsley and then surrounded by a square flower bed planted with pinks. An adjoining border grew nasturtiums, thyme, rue, sage and fuchsia.

The Lloyds divorced after World War II and sold Apple Hill in 1946.

Bunny and first husband Stacy
B. Lloyd, Jr., with son Stacy
"Tuffy" Lloyd and family pets.

Charming scenes from Apple Hill, the home that Bunny built with her first husband, Stacy Lloyd, Jr. **CLOCKWISE FROM TOP LEFT:** the house known as Apple Hill; Bunny's second greenhouse; her unique shed design built with four sides all having storage, so as to eliminate a "front to back" system; a corner of her heart-motif terrace garden; a unique handcrafted garden gate.

THE
FLOURISHING

OAK SPRING HOUSE WITH PAUL MELLON

IN 1948, RACHEL LOWE LAMBERT LLOYD MARRIED HER SECOND HUSBAND, PAUL MELLON, in the New York City living room of Foxcroft chum and decorator Sister Parish. It was the beginning of a fifty-plus-year marriage filled with great energy and the joy and challenges that any marriage brings. Paul Mellon wrote, "She brought with her two children, Stacy, nicknamed "Tuffy," and Eliza, together with a great flair and lifelong interest in gardening, building, decorating, and collecting." Clearly, for Paul Mellon, "a new influence was at work."

In anticipation of their marriage, an order was placed for dishes with the British decorator Syrie Maugham on January 26, 1948. Mellon paid $3,000 for one set of Spode china 1780, which included twelve plates, two oblong dishes, four shell-shaped dishes, one fruit dish, and two sucriers with lids and saucers. Bunny also purchased what became a favorite piece, a Victorian-style étagère, on a trip to visit Nancy Lancaster in London in 1948, according to Martin Wood in *Sister Parish: American Style*. "Never afraid to make a piece her own," remembered Susan Leopold, an Oak Spring librarian, "Mrs. Mellon lopped off the top to simplify the piece" and then proceeded to paint it for the display of her eighteenth-century hard-paste porcelain vegetable collection.

At first the Mellons were living at the farm with their four children in the Brick House, a formal, neo-Georgian-style mansion designed by famed architectural firm Delano & Aldrich and built in 1941 by Paul with his first wife, Mary Conover Brown Mellon. By Paul's own admission, the Brick House "never was a convenient house to run and had the added drawback of noisiness, stemming in large part from a central hallway and circular staircase leading all the way up to the third-floor skylight. Children's laughter and shouts were heard everywhere, and the water running in a bathtub simulated Niagara Falls down the stairwell."

Bunny's remarkable eye was on a plum site, the sweet spot of the farm, where she could create a new family home. It was an elevated ridge of land near an old stone springhouse where Bunny found architectural inspiration. "At Oak Spring there was a spring house in the lower part of the lawn, where the milk and cream were kept, and the churning done," wrote Tacie Fletcher Slater in her family memoirs,

As Told Me. "They say that the first time Grandfather Glascock saw grandmother she was coming from this spring house." The old log farmhouse where Tacie Slater's grandmother, Emily Ann Fletcher, lived was sited on this elevated ridge.

Paul Mellon added to the story: "The little nineteenth-century farmhouse at Oak Spring was placed on rollers and transported over three fields to about half a mile away, where it was put down on the edge of a Rokeby field and where it has since been the home of our secretaries."

The design of the "replacement" house, which represented Paul Mellon's "new life with Bunny and the four children," echoed the architecture and stonework of Slater's springhouse. It was sheltered by its namesake oak trees and the surrounding landscape composed of rolling farmlands lined with dry-stacked stone walls. Orchards of fruit trees dotted the landscape and a bevy of specimen trees—hawthorn and Hardy Orange—crowded in alongside. A towering, seemingly ancient beech hovered over the courtyard entranceway.

For the new house the Mellons commissioned H. Page Cross, a New York architect and family friend. The resulting house was described by Paul Mellon as "a complex of low-lying interconnecting whitewashed stone buildings with shingle roofs. The farmhouse, with its service buildings, guesthouse, and walled garden, lies nestled in gently rolling hills and is wholly in character with the surrounding countryside."

Oak Spring resembles a French hamlet, exuding a fairy-tale charm. The architect and family friend I. M. Pei commented that the Mellons' house in Upperville "is very simple—the architecture, the interior, great works of art on the walls." Billy Baldwin said of Oak Spring, "It almost looks like the house of a caretaker because it is so simple." The architecture at Oak Spring is subdued and unexpected. The main house "has the appearance of an old house which has been added on to," where one could ramble from room to room. Masses of old-fashioned flowers, and herbs shaped into topiary, were brought in from the greenhouse and displayed in the most personal way.

"Major works of art live side by side with small objects of art," a mishmash of children's drawings and "bronzes of favorite horses," Mellon said. And, finally, he rested his finger on the magic, "Bunny's quest for comfort and informality has been nurtured with care; a little natural shabbiness in an old chair cover is sometimes purposely overlooked." For Paul Mellon, the effect of his wife's efforts resulted in houses that felt "lived in and loved. More important to me than anything else, they are cheerful."

Billy Baldwin commented, "There is one thing that Paul Mellon has wherever he is, and that is total at-homeness and comfort." It was a stark contrast to the Pittsburgh house Mellon had grown up in, and he undoubtedly enjoyed the friendly and appealing atmosphere of the houses. They were all places you wanted to be.

PREVIOUS OVERLEAF: A bronze hedgehog sculpture by Jane Canfield welcomes visitors to the arbor and Formal Greenhouse beyond; detail. (Courtesy of Sotheby's Inc., © 2021.)

FACING ABOVE AND BELOW RIGHT: Steeped in English tradition, Paul Mellon was the quintessential squire of his domain, which was dominated by dogs and horses. **BELOW LEFT:** The local hunt was always welcome at Oak Spring.

FACING ABOVE: The rambling main house at Oak Spring with the "front" door discreetly tucked to the side. **FACING BELOW:** Bunny surveys her creation. **ABOVE:** Rokeby Road bifurcated the Mellon farm, with the main house on the eastern Oak Spring side and offices, working greenhouses, and airstrip occupying the Rokeby side to the west. Under the tree is a little red schoolhouse. Bunny painted this small outpost and the barns in "Rokeby red," a color that predominates in Scandinavian countries, where it is known as Falun red. **BELOW:** A pond on the grounds of Oak Spring.

Also enjoying the appealing atmosphere was Jackie Kennedy Onassis, who often rode along-side Paul Mellon in Northern Virginia's Piedmont Foxhounds and the Orange County hunt. "She's a very good rider, very, very good," Mellon told Martin Filler in 1992 for a *Vanity Fair* article titled "Cool Mellon." "She really loves it. She used to hunt with us quite a bit when the President was alive." Jackie relished the genteel, Southern style of hospitality at all of the Mellon homes. The hushed, quiet atmosphere was a welcome retreat from the grabbers and clatter of the Jackie-crazed world. Aside from the joy of spending time with friends, for Jackie, it provided the privacy that she, too, craved.

Jackie Kennedy and Bunny met in the 1950s and became close friends. Jackie admired Bunny's attention to detail and commented that "Bunny has a genius for creating an atmosphere of rarefied luxury without a hint of vulgarity," wrote Edward Klein in *Farewell, Jackie*. Bunny and Jackie's friendship began over a cup of hot tea on a Sunday afternoon at Oak Spring. "I loved your house, but I don't like mine," Jackie confided to Bunny afterward. Though Bunny was nine-teen years older than Jackie, age was no deterrent as these two kindred spirits welcomed each other's friendship. The sublime world of Bunny's houses exuded comfort and an authentic sense of style. Wrote Klein, "Among the style cognoscenti, her taste was considered to be unsurpassed."

Paul Mellon described the interior in detail:

> *The interior, under low ceilings, is full of light. The broad-planked floors, for the most part painted, sometimes plain distressed white or in patterns of two colors, emulate a method Bunny admired in Sweden years ago. . . . The furnishings [could] be loosely described as French provincial. Bunny's touch is everywhere, and throughout the house there are flowers, from tiny plants in little pots and jars to large informal arrange-ments. Informality and lightness are the keynotes which may be seen in everything from the bright printed fabrics and colorful rugs to the soft painted walls and woodwork.*

Billy Baldwin, on his first collaboration with Bunny, discovered that she was willing to take risks. "Oh, come on, Billy," she coaxed. "Let's take a chance. You aren't sure and neither am I." And, yes, they did take chances, and yes, "there were times when our choice was wrong." But Bunny was "always perfectly willing to be honest about any admission of failure, and ready to tackle the problem again. She is a very intelligent woman." And patient, too! Bunny humorously told friend and local antiques dealer Malcolm Magruder, "We don't need any clever ideas."

ABOVE: In the foyer, an early 19th-century Regency, white-painted and parcel-gilt settee rests upon the basket-weave-patterned brick floor. *The Watering Can*, c. 1913, by Roger de la Fresnaye (bequeathed to the National Gallery of Art), hangs above and is flanked by a pair of *tôle peinte* wall lights. **BELOW:** An 18th-century French provincial buffet anchors the east wall and holds, among other things, her 19th-century agate foot bath filled a large bouquet of seasonal flowers. A slatted garden chair, one of a set from her Formal Greenhouse, sits to the side.

Deeda Blair, a friend of Bunny's dating back to the Kennedy White House years, stated in the October 2014 issue of *Washington Life* magazine, "It would be impossible to describe the art collections—glorious Rothkos, Diebenkorns and a rare Nicolas de Stael—paintings hung in a simple way without frames."

A National Gallery of Art dinner celebrating Impressionist and Postimpressionist paintings lent by Russia remains an indelible memory for Deeda. "It was an explosion of color."

"'The mixture of flowers was something I never did before,'" Bunny told Deeda. "'I used real ones, including pear blossoms from trees in Virginia, tulips, wheat, and for strength, beautiful artificial poppies and sunflowers made of silk in France.' All in simple baskets on brilliant scarlet tablecloths. Everything in her life was done with knowledge, imagination, commitment and true expertise." When landscape architect Madison Cox arrived at Oak Spring for the first time, he thought he was at the wrong address. And when designer Bryan Huffman, whom Bunny nicknamed "Kissin' Cousin" and who is a coauthor of this book, arrived for a luncheon engagement, he "wondered if the side door on the approach was the front door." Both men were rescued by a butler.

The foyer set the tone and feel of the space with a floor of basket-weave pattern brick, well-worn and without a carpet. A Regency white-painted and parcel-gilt caned-back settee, usually scattered with small stacks of favored books, rested against the south wall with Roger de la Fresnaye's *The Watering Can*, circa 1913, on display above. Balancing this highly decorative ensemble was a long country table of medium-toned wood whose main focus was a basket or porcelain tub overflowing with brightly colored and scented blossoms from the gardens and greenhouses. Various objects were arranged to elicit a further look and various small paintings dotted the light cream-colored walls. To the north, the double doors exposed the magic of Bunny's famous garden with the Formal Greenhouse beyond. The remaining wall by the front door was the gathering point for the requisite accoutrements of rural life—boots, galoshes, walking sticks, garden implements, and pegs for woven baskets, jackets, hats, and binoculars. A French fruitwood chair, draped with a blanket with a woven "PM" monogram, stood nearby. The overall effect was one of supreme charm.

FACING LEFT: Hats at the ready for a trip out to the garden.
FACING RIGHT: Polished brass horse door knocker on the front door.
ABOVE: The west side of the foyer offers a typical country house atmosphere with its mix of rural accoutrements such as hats, riding boots, and woven hampers. Also shown are a Louis XV provincial bergère and a carved-elm figure of a hound nestled behind.

Bunny used the foyer table and floor as a stage for
favorite objects, books, topiaries, apples from her trees,
and her ever-present mix of colorful blossoms.

FACING: Watercolor by Snowy Campbell of the Gothic room with its elaborately carved fireplace surround. The portrait is Bunny's daughter, *Eliza Lloyd Moore*, by artist Mati Klarwein, c. 1964. **LEFT:** The same view in an earlier iteration of the room. The wallpaper was eventually removed and the room repainted in a citron green-yellow.

OVERLEAF: A set of Bunny's prized 17th-century botanical studies occupy the wall to the left, while straight on is a Cecil Beaton costume study for a flower seller in *My Fair Lady*. An 18th-century gray-painted, carved fauteuil sits by the triple set of arched Gothic windows overlooking the garden.

To the west of the foyer was the library, known as the Gothic Room owing to its rococo Gothic-style embrasures, which were joined and carved from timber on-site by the Oak Spring Farm carpenters. The scheme of the room, from the citron-infused walls to the soft-white-ground chintz with pale flowers in shades of pinks and multihues of green, was created by John Fowler of Colefax and Fowler in England and implemented by designer Paul Leonard, Bunny's in-house design guru. The room had arched Gothic windows facing north and south with her customary fitted folding shutters. The bookshelves were filled with the colorful spines of books, small paintings, sentimental bibelots, and Chinese export porcelains. There was green woven Axminster carpeting with a small geometric pattern underfoot. Above the intricate fireplace surround hung a small portrait of Bunny in her signature beret by society artist Charles Baskerville. The effect of the room was decidedly English country in feel, a nod to Paul's Anglophile predilection. The north windows faced into the famous walled garden. From this vantage point, looking toward the Formal Greenhouse, Bunny and Paul could savor its beauty and intoxicating scents. To the left, in the first of a series of outbuildings, was the Guesthouse—a fairy-tale cottage with all the luxuries necessary to pamper even the most discerning of friends.

ABOVE: Books, books, and more books. From the shelves to the overflowing coffee table, it is evident why Bunny needed her own library! The soft furnishings are covered in a cheerful yet subtle chintz that offers a light, airy balance to the deeply colored book spines. **FACING ABOVE AND BELOW:** The room served double duty, functioning as a library and as a work space for Paul Mellon, a renowned collector and breeder of champion racehorses.

ABOVE: A Regency faux-bamboo bookcase enlivens the hall outside the living room. Above it hangs Pierre Bonnard's *Still Life with Dog*, c. 1913. Doors to the dining room are seen beyond. **FACING:** This Campbell watercolor offers a frontal view of the bookcase with a collection of porcelain birds and vegetables. An American hooked rug adds to the mix.

LEFT: A bookcase purchased in London was modified and painted to occupy the breezeway off of the dining room. It is filled with Bunny's treasured 18th-century porcelain vegetables and fruits produced by Chelsea, Longton Hall, Worcester, and Meissen.
ABOVE: In the south side of the breezeway, a pair of Louis XVI fauteuils, an American rag rug, and worn painted floors add to the ambiance.

From the foyer, the light-painted, diamond-patterned floors in the main hallway beckoned the eye to the dining room, which lay at the far end of the hallway, with the visual reward of Degas's *The Riders*, circa 1885, hanging above the fireplace. This hallway to the dining room led through one of the prettiest of breezeways. It housed the famous porcelain-laden étagère, flanked by weeping fuchsia trees in faience pots, with a rag rug of multihued, deep pinkish reds that supplied balance to the colorful fruits and vegetables. Across from this vignette, facing south, French doors and windows allowed for the room to be bathed in a constant glow. An antique red wheelbarrow with pots of her favorite geraniums held forth between eighteenth-century Louis XVI fauteuils. The walls were scattered with works of various vegetables by one of her favorite artists, Madeline Hewes.

The dining room beckoned beyond—a light-filled spaced dominated by the Regency mahogany table and Regency parcel-gilt, black-painted, caned armchairs resting upon an antique needlework floral carpet. Degas's *Riders* was situated above the carved sheaf of bundled wheat that comprised the crown of the fireplace surround. Four mounted-glass photospheres anchored the corners, providing ambient light for evening meals. A large, low side cabinet, primitive in form and of light-colored wood, anchored the north wall, holding decanters in Regency parcel-gilt papier-mâché coasters along with the prized gold Kentucky Derby trophy won by the Mellon horse Sea Hero in 1993. Hanging above in a most fitting way was a long, antique, equestrian painting from Paul's substantive collection of English sporting art. The west wall near the terrace held a deep, eighteenth-century George III green-painted, concave-fronted side cabinet, above which hung a painting titled *The Melon*, by Edouard Manet, circa 1880. In between the terrace doors on the south wall hung one of Bunny and Paul's favorite equestrian pieces of art, *Riders on the Beach at Dieppe*, circa 1892, by artist René Pierre Charles Princeteau. Paul liked the horses, and Bunny the modern and free feel.

FACING: *Riders on the Beach at Dieppe*, c. 1892, by René Pierre Charles Princeteau, hung on the south wall of the dining room between the terrace doors. Bunny and Paul, who had somewhat different tastes in art, both fell in love with this painting. **ABOVE:** Édouard Manet's *The Melon*, c. 1880, hung in the dining room. (Both paintings courtesy National Gallery of Art, Washington, Collection of Mr. and Mrs. Paul Mellon.)

OVERLEAF LEFT ABOVE: View of the dining room with *The Riders*, c. 1885, by Edgar Degas, above the fireplace. A Regency mahogany pedestal table with caned chairs sits on a needlepoint carpet. The pine cabinet on the left holds various horse racing trophies from Paul Mellon's champions, one of which, Sea Hero, won the Kentucky Derby in 1993. Bunny had an incredible ability to mix different periods and styles seamlessly. **OVERLEAF LEFT, BELOW LEFT:** Note the carved relief sheaf of wheat, an insignia used by Paul Mellon for his Rokeby stables. **OVERLEAF LEFT, BELOW RIGHT:** A Madeline Hewes painting hangs above two tiers of topiaries.

TOP: The dining room table is set for lunch, with a porcelain cabbage tureen holding fresh garden flowers. Manet's *The Melon* is seen on the wall above a George III green-painted concave cabinet. **ABOVE:** A set of 18th-century, George III silver salts. **RIGHT:** A typical place setting with beautiful embroidered linens and 18th-century Chinese export plates.

CLOCKWISE FROM ABOVE LEFT: English silver-gilt owl-form condiment set. A needlepoint pillow says it all. A set of George III silver salts. An 18th-century set of Mennecy asparagus jars and a pair of 18th-century white asparagus tureens and covers. A 19th-century English fruitwood caned child's chair. A needlepoint doorstop with Bunny's Oak Spring insignia. An 18th-century French porcelain potpourri vase and cover in the form of a basket overflowing with fruit. **FACING ABOVE LEFT:** A Snowy Campbell watercolor of the hallway view of the Sunday kitchen, with a view toward the window, where just outside within easy reach was a bed of mint. **FACING ABOVE RIGHT:** A closeup view of the wood floor, painted in shades of blue. **FACING BELOW:** Bunny in her Sunday kitchen, an informal setting where she cooked and enjoyed views of her garden.

LEFT: *Still Life of Oranges and Lemons with Blue Gloves*, c. 1889, by Vincent Van Gogh hung on the south wall of the living room. **FACING ABOVE:** In the living room, Vincent Van Gogh's *Wheat Fields, Auvers*, c. 1890. In left corner, the door to a small "Bunny" bar for easy access to her pre-lunch Bloody Mary (Stoli vodka and Clamato juice). The sofa is slipcovered in yellow and white butterfly fabric from Tillett Textiles. The bookcase doors opened to reveal favorite works of art. Louis XVI painted chairs in printed linens round out the seating group. **FACING BELOW:** Close-up of Van Gogh's *Wheat Fields, Auvers*, which is now part of the Mellon Collection at the National Gallery of Art. Interestingly, when as a student at Foxcroft, Eliza Lloyd (Moore) brought friends home who asked quizzically about these colorful pictures, her response was that Da (her pet name for Paul) just buys them at the store.

John Baltimore, a favored butler, remembered that the day at the farm began with the opening of the shutters, and that meant that the windows must shine. No streaks! For Baltimore, his product of choice was Sprayway "World's Best Glass Cleaner." Dating back to 1947 and made in the USA, the foaming action and ammonia-free formula touted a streak-free shine. A Rigaud candle, the Reine de la Nuit fragrance, was positioned on a small table at the foot of the circular stairway and was lit every morning. The tiny flame flickered throughout the day, filling the interior space with its sweet fragrance.

It was a crisp, clear winter's day when Bryan Huffman first visited Oak Spring. Bryan noted, "Upon arriving for my first visit, I was struck by the understatement of it all." He was ushered into the living room by a uniformed butler in jacket and tie to await the arrival of Mrs. Mellon. A "wonderful light" poured through French doors and windows that faced east, south, and west. "The air was filled with scent from baskets of beautiful flowers from her greenhouses, and the warmth of a blazing fire." The mantel surround was carved with a leaf motif in relief, and various little treasures and postcards were tucked here and there. Two small topiaries were positioned on either side. Van Gogh's *Green Wheat Fields*, Auvers, sans frame, hung above the fireplace, and his still life, *Oranges, Lemons and Blue Gloves*, hung on the south wall to the right of the large window. In front of the fireplace, a low, French tufted bench was stacked with the day's papers—the *New York Times*, the *Washington Post*, and the *New York Post*. A straw mat covered Bunny's signature painted checkerboard floors. There were two seating arrangements of French chairs and low sofas slipcovered in her favorite Tillett's yellow butterfly print, tossed with red pillows from India. Tables were scattered with small bottles, each holding a stem or two of flowers. "The lamps were lit and the room was bathed in a magical glow," Bryan recalled. The room was "completely brilliant with its world-class art, yet so relaxed and steeped in cozy comfort, right down to the unfinished small drink tables that were made on the farm." Bryan realized that all the hype about Bunny and her impeccable eye was really a truism. "If anything," he commented, "it was an understatement!"

ABOVE: In the living room, a Louis XV green-painted provincial *bureau à gradin*. A carved Louis XVI fauteuil sits at the ready should a note need to be penned. Bunny was quite sentimental, discarding very little. Family photos, auction catalogs, bronze busts, and the ubiquitous topiary fill the surfaces. The small painting to the right of the topiary is another Madeline Hewes. Many of Hewes's works were copied as notecards for Bunny, who was an inveterate note writer. **BELOW:** Detail of view across the bureau looking towards a parcel-gilt and gray-painted bookcase holding more pieces of Bunny's extensive porcelain collection. **FACING ABOVE:** Another seating group at the far end of the living room. To the right hangs *Four Jockeys,* by Edgar Degas. **FACING BELOW LEFT:** Another view of the *Wheat Fields, Auvers*. In the lower right is Bunny's "seat" on the sofa, with her telephone close at hand. To live so comfortably and nonchalantly with world-class works of art was the epitome of the Mellon style. **FACING BELOW RIGHT:** Bunny enjoying an evening with close friend Charles Ryskamp, former director of both the Frick Collection and the Morgan Library. He was a frequent companion to both Bunny and Paul and held the honor of being godfather to Bunny's grandson Thomas Lloyd.

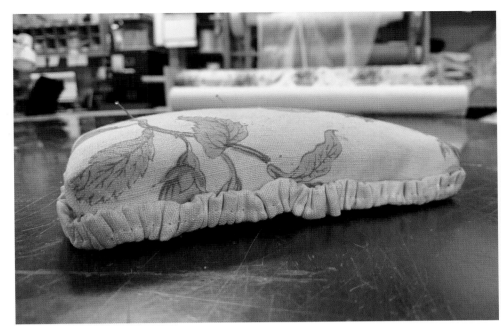

There was the "yin and yang of it all," he remembered. Amidst the casual, informal atmosphere where comfort was key, butlers reported when summoned (there was a bell under the arm of the sofa that rang in the kitchen), the silver was polished to a high sheen, surfaces glistened, and museum-quality art was displayed on walls and chairs. There were eighteenth-century pieces of porcelain fruits and vegetables, wonderfully scented cut flowers, and pots of geraniums.

"As I was taking it all in," Bryan continued, "I turned to meet Mrs. Mellon, who would come to be my friend Bunny. She had a firm, welcoming handshake and was as inviting and warm as her room—and quite tall. I was so surprised that the furniture was all so low for someone of her height." As a matter of fact, when Bryan first met legendary designer Mario Buatta, the first question Buatta asked was, "Why did Bunny have all of that doll-like-scale furniture? She was such a tall lady." Part of it goes back to the fact that she liked French furniture and that she was influenced by Billy Baldwin in the 1960s, when furniture was lower and of a smaller scale. Bryan continued, "In my ensuing visits during the many seasons, I never failed to take in that room and realize what true genius it displayed. There are so few rooms that can be so warm and inviting in winter, yet feel fresh and summery in the warmer months. I know this feeling can be achieved with a change of slipcovers, rugs, etc., but she achieved this without changing anything—same baskets of flowers, same fabrics and straw matting, yet it was transformed into a summer room. In design, this is a hard thing to accomplish. People move from house to house as the seasons rotate to get this effect."

Bunny was impressed with the work done by Custom Upholstering and Total Restorations, a furniture reupholstery shop located in nearby Marshall, Virginia. Still in operation today, their fine craftsmanship and attention to detail is what she desired in a craftsperson. "The Mellons had a particular style, and a particular style of trim that was used on all of her furnishings," interior designer Gina Krytusa of Custom Upholstering and Total Restorations told me in a phone call. The trim was cut from the same fabric and hand done. No welt, prefabricated trim or gimp could be used. A very large 5-by- 6-inch pin cushion, old and worn, still serves as an example, and fond memory, of the work that was done for Bunny.

FACING ABOVE, LEFT TO RIGHT: A Federal-style burl and figured maple table, detail. A 19th-century Napoleon III rope-twist tabouret. A Louis XVI architect's table (from her Paris apartment). MIDDLE, LEFT TO RIGHT: A Louis XV fauteuil dressed in Tillett Textiles butterflies. Carved relief over the door to the living room. Another fauteuil wears butterfly in reverse. BELOW, LEFT TO RIGHT: A George III piano stool. Bunny sets her own still life; a hidden uplight behind the folding screen offered a special glow. ABOVE LEFT: An example of the handmade style of trim that Bunny used on all her furnishings. The trim was cut from cloth and attached by hand-sewing in an uneven way to give the pieces a timeless elegance where nothing would be noticed, nothing would stand out. ABOVE RIGHT: This sample cushion remains in the shop to this day, a treasured reminder of Bunny's appreciation for expert craftsmanship.

The Oak Spring garden was built to resemble Arthur and Rachel Lowe's garden in Fitchburg where Bunny had played as a child. The slope was terraced into three levels. The first level became a broad terrace, covered with chipped pieces of slate and interplanted with fleabane daisies and thyme. On the middle terrace of the Lowe's garden there had been a playhouse where Bunny's mother had played as a child, and where Bunny, as a child, had sewn on rainy days. On the middle terrace at Oak Spring Bunny built a small, enchanting cottage and named it the "Honey House." There was a Dutch door and a clock on the end gable, which chimed the hour through the day. On the lower terrace in the Lowe's garden there had been a sandbox for Bunny to play in. At Oak Spring, Bunny planted the lower terrace with fragrant herbs and vegetables; a small School House was built nearby in the northwest corner.

Deeda Blair in *Washington Life* magazine, October 2014, a month before the Sotheby's auction of Bunny's estate, remembered the garden:

> *No gardens have ever been more captivating than Bunny Mellon's—full of totally individual approaches to herb topiaries, rare boxwood and crab apples pleached into low hedges. One was struck by a certain simplicity, serenity, creativity and understated taste, plus impeccable maintenance.*

ABOVE LEFT: Looking across the Upper Terrace towards the guesthouse. On the other side of the brick walkway, Bunny's rose garden was set in a planted grid of germander. **ABOVE RIGHT:** The garden path with thickets of lavender cascading in full bloom. **FACING:** The Honey House, a small cottage sited on the Middle Terrace in the Oak Spring garden, whose inspiration was a playhouse in her grandparents' garden in Fitchburg, Massachusetts. A clock (unseen), attached to the stone façade above the front door, chimed the hours of the day.

FACING AND ABOVE: Two views of the guesthouse bedroom wrapped in Bunny's signature toile. A Louis XVI painted bergère chair covered in Bunny blue is situated by the ceramic stove. **ABOVE:** Of note is a table draped and skirted in an antique quilt with blue fringe that she had used in her Paris apartment. Across the room is a Louis XVI beechwood bed. **LEFT:** Assorted porcelains rest on the mantel. **RIGHT:** Bunny's use of fabric on the walls with repetition on the chair.

ABOVE LEFT: View from the guesthouse. ABOVE RIGHT: Bunny, an étude in blue, in her garden. FACING ABOVE: Grandson Thomas Lloyd in front of the Basket House, enjoying the bridge and pools inspired by the stream that ran alongside the basket factory in West Rindge, New Hampshire, where Bunny spent time with her grandfather. BELOW LEFT AND RIGHT: Some of the varieties in Bunny's gardens. BELOW MIDDLE: Bunny points out aspects of the Oak Spring garden to a friend.

Also reminiscent of her childhood, Bunny added a Basket House to the west side of the lower terrace. On their road trips to Grandpa Lowe's farm in Rindge, New Hampshire, they often stopped at a basket factory in West Rindge. A stream ran just outside the factory and, to enter the factory, you had to carefully cross two wooden planks laid across the stream. In the Oak Spring garden, Bunny replicated the stream in Rindge with a pool in front and a sliver of a bridge, the width of two planks, crossing over to the door. Just like the basket factory in Rindge, there was only one door. In the pool, Bunny had jets placed just below the water's surface to create ripples just so, and a ledge for the waters to trickle over. Inside the Basket House, she placed a Georges Braque painting of a bird on one wall, echoing the birds at the New Hampshire farm, and she hung a gallery of baskets from the rafters.

ABOVE: Inside the Basket House. A Georges Braque *Bird* is prominently on display. **FACING ABOVE:** A daybed from the Paris apartment provides a spot for a languid afternoon nap. **FACING BELOW LEFT:** The beamed ceiling with an array of her prized woven baskets. **FACING BELOW RIGHT:** Bunny, in her customary circle skirt, espadrilles, gardening hat, and Schlumberger enameled bangle, gives a tour.

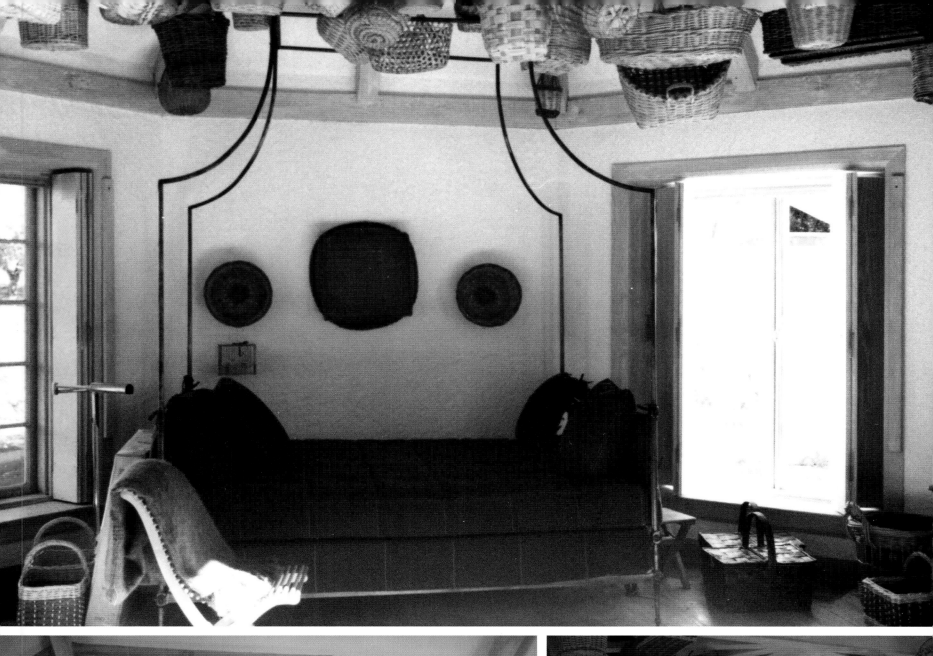

OAK SPRING FORMAL GREENHOUSE

The interior of what was the crown jewel of Bunny's garden, her Formal Greenhouse, was described by decorator Billy Baldwin: "Naturally it smells better than any greenhouse you've ever been in, and every flower is of the most extraordinary beauty, and they are loved and cared for by Mrs. Mellon herself."

The central part of the greenhouse was an octagonal room in which "there were painted trompe l'oeil shelves, and on the shelves were painted garden implements. There was even a trompe l'oeil letter from Paul Mellon giving her permission to build the greenhouse." This trick-of-the-eye painting technique was executed by French artist Fernand Renard, encapsulating depictions of Bunny's most personal treasures.

It was not exactly in need of furniture, "but it was desperately in need of one thing, and that was a table in the middle of the room." It took years but, as Billy Baldwin explains it, one day while he was shopping in New York, he found the perfect "country Louis XV painted table, which was considerably lower than the normal table height of twenty-eight inches, and this was about twenty inches in height so that one looked down on it, and whatever would be put on that table would be seen from slightly above. . . . She was overjoyed in her appreciation and enthusiasm for the table."

This was an example of her patience and attitude of doing without until the right thing came along.

ABOVE LEFT: Flowers in the Schlumberger-designed finial are being arranged. Bunny is seen under the arbor, overseeing that each stem is placed to perfection. **ABOVE RIGHT:** A Schlumberger study for the finial to sit atop the Formal Greenhouse. This would become the crowning glory of the mansard-roofed structure. **FACING:** Detail of the finial in situ.

Looking back on their years together, for the occasion of Paul and Bunny's thirtieth anniversary, May 1, 1978, Paul wrote a poem to her:

> *Thirty years have we been married*
> *Sometimes happy, sometimes harried,*
> *Sometimes joyous, sometimes blue,*
> *But still I'd marry only you.*
> *So fill the baskets up with flowers*
> *To celebrate the happy hours;*
> *Or pot pourris of sweetest scent*
> *To tell you what, to me, you've meant.*

After forty years together, Paul reflected on what she had brought to his life:

> *She . . . provided my life with a stability and security it had not known before. . . . Bunny's enthusiasm has led to the building of vacation houses at Cape Cod and Antigua, as well as her Garden Library, a beautiful church in Upperville, a dairy, an apple storage house, and sundry smaller structures. The farm and the houses in Antigua and the Cape have a "shared quality," and Bunny's touch permeates every nook and cranny, extending of course to the gardens.*

ABOVE LEFT: The low Louis XV table found by Billy Baldwin occupies the central pavilion of the Formal Greenhouse, with the arbor beyond leading to the garden. **FACING ABOVE:** Inside the central pavilion of the Formal Greenhouse with the Fernand Renard trompe l'oeil paintings. Renard, who also worked with the French design firm Jansen, collaborated with Bunny to incorporate her own things into the paintings that decorated the cabinet doors hiding her gardening tools.

ABOVE: Looking eastward, a view of the Formal Greenhouse, the moat-like pool, and the pergola cloaked with Mary Potter crabapple trees. LEFT: Fiona and Teddy Lloyd (Thomas's children) with their Labradoodle, Larry, enjoying a fall afternoon under Great-Granbunny's crabapple allée. The Formal Greenhouse is behind them. FACING: A favorite butler, John Baltimore, carries a picnic basket of refreshments for Bunny and a lucky guest. Photographed by Jonathan Becker.

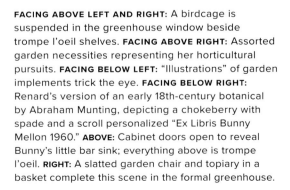

FACING ABOVE LEFT AND RIGHT: A birdcage is suspended in the greenhouse window beside trompe l'oeil shelves. **FACING ABOVE RIGHT:** Assorted garden necessities representing her horticultural pursuits. **FACING BELOW LEFT:** "Illustrations" of garden implements trick the eye. **FACING BELOW RIGHT:** Renard's version of an early 18th-century botanical by Abraham Munting, depicting a chokeberry with spade and a scroll personalized "Ex Libris Bunny Mellon 1960." **ABOVE:** Cabinet doors open to reveal Bunny's little bar sink; everything above is trompe l'oeil. **RIGHT:** A slatted garden chair and topiary in a basket complete this scene in the formal greenhouse.

ABOVE: Bunny had her gardeners make this hand-styled trellising to support nasturtiums, tomatoes, or sweet peas. **FACING:** *Teucrium fruticans*, also known as tree germander.

LEFT AND FACING BELOW:
Bunny sets a stage within
the "wedding cake"
gazebo adjacent to the
Formal Greenhouse. Her
trademark style elements
such as wicker chairs,
errant wildflowers, a straw
sun hat with ribbon, and
topiary create a respite
from the sun. The gazebo
was constructed to house
the wedding cake of
daughter Eliza and husband,
photographer Derry Moore,
12th Earl of Drogheda. Its
reflection is cast in the
moat-like pool next to the
east wing of the Formal
Greenhouse. **FACING ABOVE:**
Bunny at her radiant best
beside close friend Jackie
Kennedy at daughter Eliza's
wedding in May of 1968.
Mrs. Kennedy's Valentino
lace dress would go on to
make another appearance
at her own wedding to
Aristotle Onassis the
following October.

FACING ABOVE: On the Rokeby side of the farm, Paul and Bunny created an airstrip for their preferred mode of travel. Always generous, the Mellons allowed FEMA to use it as needed. The octagonal "welcome" structure is seen to the left. To the right of the drive are three flag poles, which held the American flag, the Oak Spring flag, and the flag of the country or state of visiting guests. **FACING BELOW LEFT:** Farm equipment shares the runway. **FACING BELOW RIGHT:** Representing the yin and yang of Bunny's high-low style is the sleek French Falcon 2000 Mellon jet (the tail number N1929Y is a reference to the year Paul graduated from Yale) pulled up to a split rail fence. **ABOVE:** Paul and Bunny share a private moment before boarding their plane.

The Oak Spring Garden Library, designed by Edward Larrabee Barnes in collaboration with Bunny Mellon, was completed in 1980. It was a gift from Mr. Mellon and designed to blend in with the surrounding landscape. A new wing, built by Thomas Beach, was added in 1997.

OAK SPRING GARDEN LIBRARY

No dusty books here. Bunny began to collect books as a young girl to "bolster" her learning and "fuel" her "growing curiosities." Books became the mainstay of her life. She hand-selected each volume and every work of art and read voraciously. As the collection grew and the shelves spilled over, she began to slide books under the bed and stack them in piles on the floor.

Like most things in Bunny's life, her love of books and a dream of having a library of her own began with her grandfather Arthur Lowe. She wrote in her journal notes that the "foundations of the Oak Spring Garden Library really began back in West Rindge, New Hampshire, on my grandfather's farm, and in Fitchburg, Massachusetts," where her "informal education in plants, design and gardens began" amidst the "roses, grape vines and raspberry bushes," and then continued at Albemarle, her father's estate.

During family travels, Bunny browsed through bookstores, "first in London and then in Paris," digging up "some of the earliest works about horticulture, by those who had invented and developed many of the now-common procedures that have both beautified and fed the world." Her books "on all aspects of gardening" were read, used and, in most cases, loved. She "owned them for decades" and "carried them around" with her. Gradually, she began to formulate her own ideas and theories from centuries-old writers—Jean de La Quintinie, John Evelyn, Paolo Bartolomeo Clarici, Daniel Loris, Jacques Boyceau, and Claude-Olivier Galimard—concluding that the older methods were better than the new. Her studies were concentrated in "Western European and American garden design, horticulture, botanical studies and voyages, published from the end of the fifteenth century through the nineteenth century . . . with an emphasis on French, Dutch and British works" that represented her "preference in garden theory." Other subject areas included "ornithology, the domestic arts, agriculture, architecture, and travel"—books that she "delighted in."

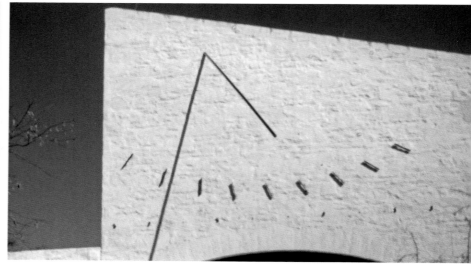

TOP ROW: Garden Library under construction. **SECOND ROW LEFT:** Pool and fountain by the library terrace. **SECOND ROW RIGHT:** When the interior space of the first wing was judged to be too narrow, this east wall was pulled down and rebuilt 18 inches wider. **THIRD ROW:** Bunny had a way of working out designs using her photographs. Left, her sketch shows placement of a large-scale sundial, and right is her photo of it completed. **FOURTH ROW:** On the left is Bunny's private area, with a dining room for her guests below and her workspace above. **FACING ABOVE:** During construction. **FACING MIDDLE LEFT:** The interior takes shape. **FACING RIGHT:** The large Rothko is unpacked and prepared for hanging. **FACING BELOW:** Old wing in the early days,

By the 1970s, after a lifetime of "collecting fine books and botanical art," it became time to decide "where to put it all—especially where it could be easily retrieved and used, when needed," a significant effort that became the beginning of the Oak Spring Garden Library.

The Mellons chose to locate the library on a "rise of land a little ways from the enclosed garden" at Oak Spring. "It sits just beyond a greenhouse, a lattice pergola of crab apples and an orchard, and looks to the west, out towards the jagged distant horizon of the Blue Ridge." Never in a hurry, Bunny had the footprint of the plan marked out with stakes. According to her gardeners, she lived with that staked outline for years. They had to mow around the stakes, sometimes carefully setting them aside and then returning them to their original placement. Bunny's library was "created slowly and painstakingly," as were her gardens. Like her father, she never considered a project done "but always evolving in the process of creation."

It was Bunny's practice to invite other professionals to collaborate with her on designs for her projects. But, make no mistake about it, whether it was a house, a garden, a church or a library—the design was always Bunny's. The Mellons commissioned Harvard-educated Edward Larrabee Barnes, noted for his modernist buildings, to design the library. Ground was broken in 1976 and the building was completed in 1980. Bunny wrote that the library is "a simple whitewashed structure reminiscent of Portuguese farmhouses, and was built by local craftsmen with fieldstones" quarried and cut on the farm. She used reclaimed wood from an old farm in upstate New York in the interiors, and "the oak for the bookcases, naturally, came from the farm."

In an interview in June 1982 for the *New York Times*, Bunny told Paula Dietz that she "wanted a modern exterior with large openings to let the outside in." The structure built during the first phase included a 75-foot main book room with floor-to-ceiling bookcases hidden behind cabinets crafted with recycled wood, and an expansive skylight. In the center of the room, beside a large, square window with views across the countryside, a Giacometti coffee table piled with stacks of books is surrounded by two skirted sofas slipcovered in off-white and an assortment of chairs. Probably one of Rothko's largest creations dominates the east wall and fills the room with bright hues of yellows and oranges. Underground stacks and a book process room are directly beneath the book room. There are also a small kitchen and Bunny's workroom "office" in a fairy-tale-shaped cubicle tower.

Naturally, the next step was to catalog the library. Owing to her dream for there to one day be a tree-pruning school at Oak Spring, it probably came as no surprise to her family and friends that she first published *An Oak Spring Sylva: A Selection of the Rare Books on Trees in the Oak Spring Garden Library* in 1989. The collection was described by Sandra Raphael and dedicated to Bunny's grandfather, Arthur Houghton Lowe (1853–1932). "Grandpa Lowe," had been her inspiration for the library, as with almost everything else in her life. In her preface, Bunny offered

ABOVE: Great-grandson Teddy Lloyd stands below Granbunny's Rothko.
BELOW: The Rothko rests in place before being hung. Skylights offered natural illumination for the deep yellows and oranges of the painting.

OVERLEAF: The evolved style of the old wing.

a peek into the cherished times that she spent with her "New Hampshire grandfather, . . . who encouraged this enthusiasm" and led her "through woods and up mountains," and took her on trips to Concord, Massachusetts, "to learn and study the world of Thoreau, Emerson, and Hawthorne," memories that contributed "to the beginning of the Oak Spring Garden Library." Today, the catalogues serve as the finest tour of the library.

An Oak Spring Pomona: A Selection of the Rare Books on Fruit in the Oak Spring Garden Library, also described by Sandra Raphael, rolled off the presses in 1990. In the preface, Bunny wrote that "Fruit—the subject of the second volume of the Oak Spring Garden Library catalogues—takes up a larger space on the shelf than some of its companions." Bunny gave us 276 pages on her second-favorite topic—fruit—and on one of her favorite hobbies—pruning.

In 1997, she introduced An *Oak Spring Flora Flower Illustration from the Fifteenth Century to the Present Time: A Selection of the Rare Books, Manuscripts and Works of Art in the Collection of Rachel Lambert Mellon*. This volume was dedicated to her friend Jacqueline Bouvier Kennedy Onassis. During the Kennedy presidency, the two friends transformed floral management at the White House—building a flower room next to the Rose Garden, hiring new florists, and mixing garden flowers grown at the new greenhouse with hot house flowers in arrangements that were looser and freer in form.

Bunny opened *Flora* with another tribute to her grandfather featuring an illustration of the first flower book that he gave her, a revised edition of *Flower Guide: Wild Flowers East of the Rockies*, and describes flowers as "the paintbox of garden design," and notes that flowers can "create a sense of peace and simplicity."

The last catalog was published in 2009, *An Oak Spring Herbaria: Herbs and Herbals from the Fourteenth to the Nineteenth Centuries*, and was dedicated to her "dearest friend and daughter, Eliza Lloyd Moore," who had passed away the year before. In the foreword Bunny describes the "remarkable books and artwork on herbs and herbals" in the collection and lists the common herbs that "grow wild" around the library in the summer months: "common mullein, dandelion, plantain, poke weed, and yarrow."

This is "a working library where mystery, fascination, and romance contribute to centuries of the art of gardening as a source of discovery," wrote Bunny.

FACING: T. J. Hunter's 18th-century engraving *The Great American Aloe* anchors this grouping. **ABOVE:** A 17th-century Jan van Kessel still life of moths, insects, and a parma violet.

OVERLEAF LEFT ABOVE: A bleached, crude farm table with simple stretcher support holds a mix of rare books and a topiary in a painted tub. **OVERLEAF LEFT, BELOW LEFT:** On a side wall in the new wing hangs *Fritillaria pallidiflora*, a 17th-century French school oil painting from a pharmacy in the Loire Valley; detail. **OVERLEAF LEFT, BELOW RIGHT:** Table detail. **OVERLEAF RIGHT:** A library ladder rests against the whitewashed walls next to a collection of paintings and tables laden with a selection of horticultural books.

Susan Leopold, PhD, a Mellon librarian from 1999 to 2010, who worked with Mrs. Mellon on the writing and illustrations for *Herbaria*, described Bunny as a woman who was "ahead of her time" and who had a "strong sense of style and intuition." Susan described the library as a "feminine" library, and remembered it as "a place you wanted to be in and explore." She recalled that "the books were tended like a garden." Bunny was "focused on the beauty of the setting" and was "interested in creating a home for the books, and a spirit of the people the books were about."

In contrast to "male" libraries, which are often dark and foreboding spaces lined with heavy mahogany bookshelves, Bunny embraced space and filled it with light. Uplifting and expansive interiors welcome the light through well-placed windows and skylights. Bookshelves constructed of reclaimed, weathered wood line the walls. Bunny "added little green boxes—bright colors—to bring an element of light to the shelves," Susan reflected. The furnishings echo the same lightness in feeling and attitude.

Bunny "didn't organize her books in alphabetical order, or according to the Dewey Decimal System," Susan noted. She had "a deep vision," which was the "art of the collection." The books were arranged in an appealing manner "to awaken thoughts and ideas," and according to "her own themes and placement" so you "could go to any section and discover." Bunny had her own categories; "she didn't look to anyone for advice." The "teaching materials were located upstairs" in the two-story library, "where the fairies lived," along with "the fairy tale collection, the children's books, the big flower books, and the plant explorers, which were all organized by region." Downstairs were the "travelers, the nautical, and the faraway, along with the garden and floral design books." There is an "art to placement," Susan said admiringly, and "she had it."

"The female elements of tending—placement—light—comfort—and beauty" all played a role in Bunny's library, creating a welcoming sense of being for the books, art and objects as well as for the visitor, scholar and plant person. There are worlds awaiting discovery.

Listing Bunny's legendary garden achievements, which included the Potager du Roi at Versailles and the very beautiful, useful and distinguished White House Rose Garden, Deeda Blair exclaimed that Bunny's "interests ranged far beyond. Among them is a lasting legacy: the creation of a great horticultural library with over 3,500 rare books and manuscripts beginning in the fifteenth century, together with over 10,000 reference works."

It was a rare experience to be invited to the library during Bunny's lifetime. Prince Charles became one of the lucky ones when he visited Oak Spring in 1985 with the Princess of Wales. Martin Filler wrote in "Cool Mellon," *Vanity Fair*, April 1992, that the Prince "came away raving" about the library "and illuminated books by William Blake." Paul Mellon added that the Prince "got along with Bunny very well, because he's interested in gardening and books and flowers." And that feeling was greatly reciprocated.

Bunny's office in the library tower. Her sawhorse table is strewn with letters, files, books, and catalogs, all pertaining to her horticultural endeavors. The "desk" chair is slipcovered with her standard ruffled trim from which a loosely gathered skirt falls. The basket to the right holds architectural and garden plans, while a low Louis XV bench provides a surface for books along with a piece of fabric being studied as a possibility for its covering.

OVERLEAF LEFT: Across the workroom, an Eliza Lloyd Moore collage commands the wall above a simple wooden bench. **OVERLEAF RIGHT ABOVE:** A pillow-strewn settee sits next to the spiral stair. **BELOW LEFT:** Eliza's 1964 portrait, which originally hung in the Gothic room of the main house. **BELOW RIGHT:** Detail of the Eliza Lloyd Moore collage.

PAGES 122–123: A selection of chairs from the library. The focal point of the library dining room is the blue-and-white-tiled Swedish stove. A bleached octagonal table with French side chairs rounds out the ensemble.

ABOVE: Braque-style bird weather vane flies over the main entrance of the Memory House. ABOVE RIGHT: Bunny designed her interior landscapes to celebrate views of the outside. MIDDLE: The garden beautifies the northern entrance. BELOW: Bunny wished for the Memory House to embody vignettes from her various homes along with Lambert/Lloyd/Lowe family memorabilia.

THE MEMORY HOUSE

Bunny's daughter, Eliza Lloyd Moore, an accomplished artist with an infectious spirit of joy and creativity, was brought home to the farm following serious injuries from an accident in New York City. There she spent the last ten years of her life. While trying everything imaginable to restore her daughter's health, Bunny turned her thoughts to what would become her last building project—a small house built on a rise of land north of the library. She named it the Memory House, as it was intended to be the repository for all Lambert-Lloyd Family memorabilia and Eliza Lloyd Moore's extensive works of art, as well as Bunny's final stage set, a place where favored pieces from her various residences and collections would be on display. "Like most people make photo albums, she organized her life and put it in a house," said Okey Turner, the collaborator to whom she entrusted the design of the structure. In a phone call with me, he offered keen insight into Bunny's design process.

They met at the library. "It was very informal," Okey said. "Mrs. Mellon, now in her nineties, said that she assumed I'd be helpful." After a brief conversation, Bunny asked him to "go home and do a drawing." He returned with "a sketch of a building like the library," which is what he thought she had in mind. It wasn't.

"I want something that looks more like a farm building. Go around the farm and look for inspiration," she told him. "She had a dove weather vane that she wanted to mount on top of the Memory House, so the cupola was built for the weather vane." Okey said that Bunny was "mostly interested in the details," and told him, "an inch makes a difference." When asked if it was true that the roof was raised after it was completed, Okey replied, "Yes, we adjusted it a bit higher."

Bunny had a stand of oak trees on the farm removed, milled, and stacked in drying barns to season. Okey explained, "It's much better to air-dry the wood, which normally takes two to three years." He added, "In the old days, the wood would be cut a year ahead of building the house to let the wood dry out."

Bunny approached the designing and building of the Memory House like a blank canvas. "Mrs. Mellon hated air-conditioning," Okey remembered. "She insisted the rooms be well ventilated." Each window had a layer of shutters, screens and windows of regular glass. "There were three to four things to open and close on each one of the windows," he added. The "individual panes of glass have special doors that can be opened separately." Okey accomplished this by making a frame around each pane of glass and placing it in the sash so that each pane could individually be opened and closed. Even the trim around the doors and windows had to be a certain way.

Bunny often visited the building site and was always appreciative of the work being done.

She and Okey had many discussions where ideas were floated and tossed around while Bunny figured things out for herself. "She didn't like the idea of an expert coming in," Okey said. "No experts from the National Gallery of Art were welcome. She did not accept expert advice. She didn't want anyone telling her what to do. She'd decide on her own." She was "wary of architects," and felt that "architects want to do things their own way, they have their own vision. Mrs. Mellon would not listen to anyone else."

The interior formula echoed Bunny's lifelong love of painted floors and light, bright spaces. As her life was coming to its natural end, she became even more spare and modern, eschewing comfortable clutter and seeking only the finest, simplest, and purest of elements for this, her final project.

TRINITY EPISCOPAL CHURCH

Trinity Episcopal Church, located in the village of Upperville, Virginia, in the foothills of the Blue Ridge Mountains, was designed and built by Bunny and funded by the Mellons. She was on-site, oversaw the building of the church and had the last word. The Gothic-style front doors, adorned with cast-iron latches and door pulls crafted in the whimsical shape of a horse's head—a nod toward the local equestrian gentry, and Bunny's way of creating an experience—open into a small vestibule paneled in dark wood, with a cool-to-the-touch stone floor. Resplendent, just-picked seasonal flowers, artfully arranged in an airy manner, often grace a side table. Overhead, the dark-stained main support beam appears off-center. It is. Bunny intentionally placed the beam off-center as a symbolic gesture that God alone is perfect, fostering a worshipful sense of the divine. The significance of the off-center beam cannot be overstated. It is tangible evidence of Bunny's design ethos, her elusive mystique summed up in her statement "nothing should be noticed . . . nothing should stand out." These seemingly small, yet painstakingly thoughtful, symbolic details, made up the whole of Bunny's aesthetic, as she used the timeless design elements of harmony, balance, scale and proportion to curate her vision and sense of style.

Window number one of six stained glass windows in the nave, designed by Joep Nicholson of the Netherlands. The story of creation is pictured, beginning with the figure of God seated on a rainbow, Eve offering the apple to Adam, and the departure of Adam and Eve from the Garden of Eden.

THESE WINDOWS ARE GIVEN IN MEMORY OF
MARY CONOVER MELLON
BY HER FAMILY AND FRIENDS
DESIGNED BY JOEP NICOLAS A.D. 1959

ABOVE: The dedication window, depicting an oak tree, was designed by Rowan LeCompte. **FACING ABOVE LEFT:** The third church building to stand on this site was designed by Bunny Mellon and H. Page Cross. Construction was done entirely by local craftsmen. **ABOVE MIDDLE:** Cross above the altar is constructed of rough-hewn barn timbers. **ABOVE RIGHT:** An interior lantern executed by the firm of P. A. Fiebiger of New York City, who forged the interior and exterior ironwork and the intricate chandeliers and grilles in the church.

MIDDLE LEFT: Angel of Peace lantern, an exterior tower light, was designed by H. Page Cross and forged by Paul Fiebiger. **MIDDLE RIGHT:** On a corner of this hexagonal oak pulpit designed and hand-carved by Heinz Warneke, is a carved representation of Martin Luther. **BELOW LEFT:** A small altar in the south transept. **BELOW RIGHT:** The wooden entrance door leading from the covered walkway to the vestibule was salvaged from the second Trinity Church building.

WASHINGTON, D.C. HOUSES

THE MAIN RESIDENCE IN WASHINGTON, D.C. was 3041 Whitehaven Street, located near the Naval Observatory. With its stately, redbrick Georgian exterior, this house more closely suited Paul Mellon and his love of all things English. It boasted ten bedrooms and nine and a half baths and had a lovely rear garden with a large covered terrace.

The interiors tended more to city formality; yet, with all that Bunny touched, it had that certain *je ne sais quoi* charm. Degas and Cezanne mingled with painted floors, a large trompe l'oeil bookcase with faux marble surrounds, floral Portuguese needlepoint carpets, and soft floral chintz against crosshatched walls. A portrait of Andrew Mellon, Paul's father, Secretary of the Treasury, Ambassador to the Court of St. James and creator of the National Gallery of Art, held a prominent perch above the fireplace in the drawing room. Fresh flowers delivered from the Virginia farm filled baskets and small porcelain containers throughout. Lowestoft and Chinese export porcelain saucers, replete with matchbooks displaying the name "Rokeby Stables Upperville," with the sheaf of wheat insignia embossed in gold, served as ashtrays. Paul Mellon's red English post box found a prominent spot in the welcoming foyer and served as the center of his flurry of correspondence.

John Baskett, collaborator with Mr. Mellon for his book *Reflections in a Silver Spoon*, remembers the house fondly. He was always greeted with a warm welcome from Murray, a longtime butler. Murray would chide Baskett as his bags (including a large trunk) were presented in the foyer: "Ah, Mr. Baskett, I see you've brought the coffin with you."

Baskett recalls the house served as a pied-à-terre for the Mellons, with Bunny making minimal appearances—usually only for social duties such as hosting dinners at the National Gallery and luncheons for friends, including Prince Charles. It also served as a gathering spot for important family occasions, such as the post-baptismal luncheon for grandson Thomas Lloyd.

The Mellons also owned the house next door, Number 3055, where Baskett organized Paul Mellon's collection of English pictures into "some sort of order" and hung "over one hundred French paintings that later went to the National Gallery."

Three watercolors by Snowy Campbell. **PREVIOUS OVERLEAF:** The living room at 3041 Whitehaven Street, detail. Displayed above the mantel is a portrait of Paul Mellon's father, Andrew Mellon, secretary of the treasury to three American presidents, ambassador to the Court of St. James, and founder of the National Gallery of Art.

FACING: Works by Degas and Cezanne enhance the inviting atmosphere of this charming sitting room, where cheerfully mixed layers of pattern can be seen. The walls feature one of Bunny's preferred crosshatch methods of paint applications; detail. **ABOVE:** Bunny elevated the view of the room with this hand-painted secretary, replete with Mellon family personal objects.

FACING AND ABOVE LEFT: Fresh flowers snipped from Bunny's gardens and loosely arranged in her preferred method presented eye-catching displays. ABOVE RIGHT: Murray, the butler at Whitehaven Street. BELOW LEFT: BELOW LEFT: An umbrella stand was customary in Bunny's entryways. BELOW RIGHT: Paul Mellon's English-style mailbox held pride of place in the entrance hall.

Scenes of the dining room. **FACING:** A special porcelain tureen, one of a collection, rests upon the demilune cabinet. **ABOVE:** Of note are the painted chairs, which reappear in the Paris apartments. As collections grew, they were dispersed to other residences. **LEFT:** Bunny's favored ceramic cabbage is showcased. **BELOW RIGHT**: An Asian-inspired wicker sedan chair adds a bit of exoticism to the room.

OVERLEAF: Readied with sumptuous luncheon preparations, the scene has been set for the all-important visit of a royal guest, HRH Prince Charles. The chairs from the previous page are now mixed with a set of 18th-century George III caned dining chairs with cushions.

These Campbell watercolors offer glimpses into Bunny's welcoming decorative style. She favored canopy beds, often festooned with fabrics that complemented the art. She used printed fabrics much in the manner one does with toile, employing them in the overall décor, even on the walls. Fireplaces were a staple in these rooms, paired with French bergères.

NEW YORK CITY TOWNHOUSE

125 EAST 70TH STREET

IN 1942, WHILE IN THE ARMY AND MARRIED TO HIS FIRST WIFE, Paul Mellon rented a century-old brownstone "on the site of my present house on East 70th Street." At first, the house was used only once or twice a month when he and Mary were in the city, but after Paul was stationed at Fort Hamilton in Brooklyn it became more of a home.

When Bunny became Mrs. Paul Mellon, she began to make her own imprint on the brownstone. During her first year of marriage, on January 24, 1949, she placed an order for household furnishings for East 70th Street with Syrie Maugham that included one basket of fruit, $700; one small blue velvet stool, $250; one butterfly marble top table, $495; one French 18th-century étagère, $645; one pair bullrush wall lights, $450; one small black lacquer table, $195; four easy chairs as per London estimate at $140 each plus freight and duty.

On March 14, 1949, Mrs. Mellon's secretary, Elizabeth Rye, wrote to Syrie Maugham and enclosed a check of $1,295—for a white-painted bedside table to go to Virginia, $150; a white-painted bookcase for the New York townhouse, $750; and a Louis XV table with shelves, $395. Ms. Rye noted to Maugham that "Mrs. Mellon was in such a rush the last day she was here that she asked me 'would I please write to you to tell you to go ahead with the copy of the red sofa, making it one inch shorter in the leg.'" She ended the letter by saying that Mrs. Mellon would "appreciate it if you will not sell the two white cupboards which you have hidden away for her."

On November 14, 1950, the estate of Hobart G. Erwin at 15 East 57th Street sold a "small antique Franklin stove—second hand, circa 1810—$30" to Bunny. And a few months later, on January 15, 1951, Syrie Maugham wrote to Mrs. Rye with what she described as "boring detail" to say that the Mellons' account was "up to date except for a pair of balloon wall lights that Mrs. Mellon still has." She wasn't sure whether she wanted them or not. "Perhaps when she gets to New York and looks at them again she will be able to decide because if she doesn't want them I have a client at Mount Kisco who would like them."

When the time came to raze the existing structure, which Paul Mellon referred to as "bedraggled," and build a replacement, the Mellons commissioned architect

PREVIOUS OVERLEAF: The original New York living room décor, with yellow walls as captured by Snowy Campbell. Bunny used a combination of soft furnishings and French chairs from varying periods in soft pastels to set off the artworks. Her trademark topiary is seen to the left.

LEFT: The living room, now painted in a soft peachy-pink crosshatch, is shown in a later iteration. The centerpiece of the room is the John Singer Sargent painting above the fireplace. The painting originally hung in the study but was moved at Bunny's direction and dictated the new color scheme. **ABOVE:** Small enameled and jeweled boxes float with a small bouquet on a modern table.

FACING: *Miss Beatrice Townsend* (1870–1884), painting by John Singer Sargent. Miss Beatrice was the sixth of seven children of New York attorney and politician John Joseph Townsend and his wife, Catherine, a friend of the artist. Sargent's earliest works were of children, often with a favored pet. Bunny found the painting captivating, marveling at the child's self-confidence as she stares straight into the eyes of the viewer. (Sadly, Miss Townsend died two years later at the age of fourteen.) The painting was gifted to Paul by his father, Andrew Mellon, and is now at the National Gallery of Art. **ABOVE:** Bunny at ease in her setting.

H. Page Cross to design the new townhouse and hired building contractor William Crawford, Inc. During an interview, Crawford's grandson Richard Hanington said, "Page Cross advised Mr. Mellon, 'You need to build the house on two lots—not just one.' So, Mr. Mellon bought the lot next door that had been owned by baseball player Hank Greenberg. It became a double lot, and Cross continued."

Hanington added, "Cross also advised Mr. Mellon that he needed to build a two-story mansard roof and Mr. Mellon said, 'No—to stick to the single.'" Cross replied, "It's fine with me if you want to live in a house that is architecturally incorrect." Mr. Mellon changed his mind and built the second-story mansard.

For the ironwork, they turned to Paul Fiebiger, of P. A. Fiebiger Iron Works in New York City, a firm that dated back to May 1900. (Fiebiger also crafted the ironwork for Oak Spring and Trinity Episcopal Church.) Paul Fiebiger crafted the railings and fences along East 70th (where they can be seen today) and the interior staircase. Dick Hanington reported that "Page Cross copied the house staircase from one he had seen in a movie. He and Crawford went to the movie several times, and Cross used the sketch he drew."

"Cross's talented designer, Arthur Taylor, designed the stair railings," all the details, and "every hammer blow," according to Fiebiger's son, Joseph, who said that he "grew up on the Trinity Commission."

"I love our house," Bunny told fashion writer Eugenia Sheppard during an interview in 1966 for the *New York Herald Tribune*, in the soft voice that matched Bunny's honey blond hair brushed back from her face and turned up in a flip. Sheppard had to compete with the ongoing hum of construction. The photo caption reads, "Mrs. Paul Mellon." That's it. Bunny was keeping a promise—"luncheon and a first chance before anyone else, to look at her new townhouse," Sheppard wrote. The house, Sheppard noted, was as "personal as a portrait."

Bunny described the inside of the new white town house at 125 East 70th Street in NYC as "very, very unfinished, like an unfinished French Impressionist painting" and added that she was "so lucky to have Hank Greenberg [the famous baseball player] as my neighbor. He's just a saint. The workmen wake him up at 7:30 every morning."

Bunny asked John Fowler and Imogen Taylor of Colefax and Fowler in London to decorate the house. Taylor explained to Mitch Owens, editor at *Architectural Digest*, that Fowler "never wanted to leave England. He liked his own bed," and that his "sole top-to-bottom American project was conducted entirely through the post working from measurements taken out there and with photographs of empty rooms. It was an amazing thing to do—and not very satisfactory, really."

Billy Baldwin later described the house as "an amazingly attractive French town house" that did not disappoint. The small gated courtyard entrance, the pruned topiaries in wooden tubs, and the dark green door sparked a memorable first impression.

Although the townhouse boasted an elevator, this interior stairwell, which spanned all the floors, created visual drama. The walls are covered in a linen toile fabric, while paintings from the Mellon collection add bright punches of color. The wrought-iron railing was crafted by Paul Fiebiger, a New York ironmonger who went on to do all of Bunny's ironwork in her various houses and projects, including Trinity Episcopal Church in Upperville. The stair empties into the hall below, and beyond is a glimpse of the corner banquette designed by Paul Leonard.

OVERLEAF: A vision in blue! The dining room's cobalt crosshatch walls were designed by the legendary John Fowler, whose eponymous firm Colefax and Fowler created many of Bunny's design schemes in England. They were then implemented by Bunny's personal designer and painter Paul Leonard and his partner Bill Strom. Apple-green bergères anchor the corners and echo the Givenchy-designed tablecloth with Bunny's Oak Spring insignia embroidered in the corners. Between the terrace doors hangs Edouard Manet's *George Moore in the Artist's Garden*, c. 1879, now part of the Mellon Collection at the National Gallery of Art.

During Sheppard's interview with Bunny, the hammering continued, and Sheppard took note that Bunny called each of the workmen by name. They met in the drawing room. Yellow curtains finished with handmade tassels complemented the glazed yellow walls. There was a large piano at the end of the room that Bunny commented on as she twirled a lengthy strand of beads wrapped in triplicate around her neck, "We know it's too big, but we like music." Sheppard was surprised at the rug—a "modern Portuguese and it cost less than $400.00," Bunny had commented. The silk sofa pillows were personalized with painted images of topiary trees.

Paul Leonard, a theatrical stage designer turned designer-in-residence for the Mellon family, "painted the dining room walls to look like heavy, textured silk," Bunny told Sheppard. "There was lighting at the base of the white louvered shutters that glowed like supplementary candles." The wall painting technique was selected to complement the art, in this case the painting *George Moore*, by Edouard Manet.

At the time of the interview, decorators Paul Leonard and partner Bill Strom were in the dining room "up on step ladders hanging the bright blue and off-white striped silk draperies" that had just arrived from England. The curtains were made in London with "specially designed silk made in Lyon." Imogen Taylor described the curtains in her book *On the Fringe: A Life in Decorating* as "unlined silk faille curtains" with a "certain style" and sown from "silk specially woven and the poles from which they are hung specially made, and everything totally hand-crafted." The dining room—and the curtains—were a triumph. Taylor noted that when Jackie Kennedy "moved into her apartment at 1040 Park Avenue [she] wanted some simple curtains like the ones we had made for Bunny." The chandelier was from Syrie Maugham.

Paul Leonard told *Architectural Digest* in August 1981, "I like to create settings for something wonderful to happen in." A hands-on artist, Leonard was willing "to take on just about any task that has to do with living spaces, be it wiring and plumbing, furniture designing, curtain-making, bricklaying, gardening, or running off a party for a hundred." And that included being sent by Bunny to London to be trained by designer John Fowler, of Colefax and Fowler.

Leonard considered the painted floors to be "his trademark," a technique that he "borrowed from the Swedes, who paint floors to look like marble." Leonard "scored, sanded, and painted the wood floors in geometric designs with an oil paint base topped by casein paint and finished with beeswax."

In Bunny's sparse written notes on the house, she wrote that the objects on the fireplace mantel were "designed specially by Jean Schlumberger of gold and lapis." The table settings included a lettuce service, an English dessert service, a Chantilly service and a tobacco-leaf service.

ABOVE: View into the dining room. **BELOW LEFT:** Bunny always maintained a room for flower arranging. Note the retractable cabinet door, which serves double duty as a platform for assembling the stems. **BELOW RIGHT:** Watercolor by Snowy Campbell of the dining room dressed for a dinner with part of Bunny's extensive collection of 18th-century Chinese export tobacco leaf porcelain.

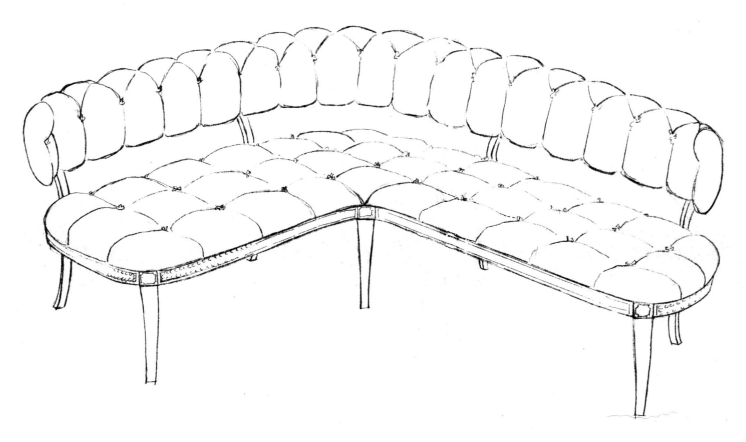

FACING ABOVE: Table detail with hand-painted porcelain fruit in a dish. FACING BELOW: Paul Leonard's drawing of the banquette, which changed in modest ways during the design and construction process. ABOVE: Bunny's innovative corner banquette, designed by Paul Leonard, is overhung by a group of paintings by Italian artist Giorgio Morandi. RIGHT: Morandi specialized in still life and is noted for his tonal subtlety in depicting simple objects such as vases, bottles, bowls, and flowers.

Bunny made a rough list of important items in the house. On the first floor, George Stubbs's painting Zebra was displayed in the entryway and there was a "garden corridor with basket collection." Over the mantel in Paul Mellon's office was "Miss Beatrice Townsend by [John Singer] Sargent, once owned by Paul's father, Andrew Mellon." There were Morandi paintings in the hallway, and the overscale "toile de Jouy with paintings by Bonnard" covered the walls of the central staircase. "Bonnard was very fond of hanging his work on printed fabric," Bunny wrote.

On the second floor, the "original design for the shape of walls and ceilings was done by John Fowler of London, who hoped to come and finish details but did not like the trip across the Atlantic."

Other appointments included an "antique armoire to hold vases and tools, Cezanne pears and papier mache," wrote Bunny, and a small chair from Syrie Maugham. The floor was painted in a "diamond pattern, to look like an old Italian villa." Bunny used scale, pattern and color on the floor designs to link the rooms, creating a cohesive whole.

Mitch Owens had the good fortune of meeting Paul Leonard. In Owens's column, "The Aesthete," he wrote:

> *Leonard described the process of creating the floors for the Mellons, which "appeared aged even when they were brand-new." The multiple hand-applied glazes and careful sanding and scraping that revealed some of the underlying layers were techniques that Fowler and George Oakes—then a director at the firm and one of the twentieth century's most talented decorative artists—taught Leonard and Strom when they were flown to London for a tutorial. "The boys," as Fowler called them, also employed a metal tool in their work, lightly scoring the wood planks to achieve a trompe l'oeil effect that suggested inlaid stone.*

FACING: A Snowy Campbell unfinished watercolor rendition of the New York entry hall. The pedestal holds a *tôle peinte* and faux marble model of a plant. Suspended above is a Louis XVI–style gilt bronze lantern. Note Bunny's typical shutters in upper right quadrant.
ABOVE: Bunny's magical floral touch in front of the George Stubbs *Zebra* painting, c. 1763, which is now at the Yale Center for British Art.

ABOVE: Snowy Campbell renderings of details from Bunny's bedroom. Bunny's style is apparent, from the French fauteuil and Louis XVI carved, lyre-back side chair to the delicate blue geometric carpet and the simple off-white linen-skirted table filled to capacity with "treasures."
BELOW: A still-life tableau created and photographed by Bunny.
FACING: Bunny's key elements are in place in this watercolor of her bedroom. Curtains and bed hangings in the same fabric. Walls in a soft-blue and off-white stripe. A blue bergère chair holds her talisman "Braque bird," which was found in some form at all of her properties.

Bunny used the transformative powers of treillage to hide the ugly scar that was exposed on the side of the building next door during the construction process. Elsie de Wolfe wrote in *The House in Good Taste*, "A knowledge of the history of treillage and an appreciation of its practical application to modern needs is a conjurer's wand—you can wave it and create all sorts of ephemeral constructions." What was once an eyesore became a structure of architectural beauty through the process of weaving strips of green wood in a crisscross pattern. Niches and trellises were woven into the basket-weave pattern. The walls of a corridor that led to the terrace were also covered in lattice strips of wood woven together like baskets.

Bunny described the design of 70th Street as "very practical" and that "without changing a single partition it could be divided into four separate apartments," like Hank Greenberg's house next door. "I don't believe we're living in a time when anything should be built that can't be converted."

Eugenia Sheppard, in her article for the *New York Herald Tribune*, seemed at a loss on how to label Bunny's style. It's "neither all-American or all-European. It is neither classical or contemporary, if by contemporary you mean the pop art world. Let someone else supply dimensions and statistics. It is simply what every woman is always longing for in the back of her head, a little piece of beauty and perfection, far away from the rest of the world, behind a dark green gate."

On November 10, 1967, family friend and "Kissin' Cousin" Nancy Lancaster typed a letter to Bunny on her Haseley Court stationery. "Page Cross took me to your house," she began, "in a downpour. It was lovelier than ever and flowers not needed. I love the curtains in the drawing room and the rug is the most beautiful I have ever seen." And, in her cheeky way, she continued, "As I know you want me to be perfectly frank, the only thing I did not like were the two pineapples you bought from us in the hall. They seemed unworthy of the Stubbs and too gimmicky." The other thing she didn't like was the "orange velvet on the seat, [which] could be improved by something older and less startling." She continued, "The chintz in the bedroom above yours drove me to a frenzy of envy. Could I ever have a pattern of it? I adored your bedroom more than ever and nearly stole the gold dressing table set in the powder room." For a finishing touch, she fired off a compliment: "What lovely taste you have, every detail perfection."

Garnering sympathy, Nancy Lancaster reported that the day she returned home, she "fell from a ladder and broke my wrist and it will be in plaster for six weeks." Then she closed with a pitch: "I am going to Jamaica on 31st January and to the Mill Reef Club in Antigua from 15th February for ten days, so please let me see your house as I am told it is the best thing done in this century." Mrs. Lancaster signed her missive, "With love and please use this as your base whenever you come to England, Nancy."

PREVIOUS OVERLEAF: A Bunny tableau set in the garden. Garden walls covered in intricately patterned wooden treillage creates a bucolic feeling, belying the reality that this is in a New York City neighborhood.

ABOVE: Bunny entertains on the side terrace. **BELOW:** One of four identical Italian obelisks anchors a corner of the center bed in the garden.

CAPE COD HOUSE

BUNNY DESCRIBED THEIR HOUSE AT OYSTER HARBOR ON CAPE COD AS "A LOW WINDSWEPT SHINGLED BUILDING BY THE SEA" that has "spread with the years, until it has made a courtyard on the north side." Whimsical weather vanes and finials added a light touch, crowning the pinnacles of numerous rooftops in "a simple landscape created by the sea and wind, rather than man." Bunny noted, "the silence is broken rarely by anything more than a Sea-Bird's cry or waves on the outer shore." From her journal:

> *August 10, 1980. This first day is a clear—cool blue—with sea and sky all around. A song sparrow sings on the olive outside my window. He is always there from early morning until dark. Beyond the tree the boat is tied to the dock. For the moment the sparrow and slight sound of water are the only things breaking the stillness.*

The Main House, designed by H. Page Cross, was built in the 1950s on a bluff overlooking Sepuit River, surrounded by dunes, beach grass and rosa rugosa, with views toward Dead Neck Island, which the Mellons preserved as a bird sanctuary, and Nantucket Sound.

Bryan Huffman observed that the interior followed in the typical Bunny Mellon style. Painted and patterned floors ran throughout. The ceilings were kept intentionally low so as to create an intimate, cottage-like atmosphere. Soft and light pastel colors suffused the walls, allowing a perfect backdrop for many works from the Mellon art collection, including a wonderful Dufy above the mantel in the dining room. Many of the floors had soft, nubby and natural rugs, along with plenty of antique hooked rugs.

Bryan also remembered that the foyer had the typical Mellon accoutrements of pegs and hooks for hosting the utilitarian umbrellas, baskets, beach bags and hats along with an ever-present croquet set alongside a weathered tall-case clock. Cushions and baskets for treasured four-legged friends were scattered about the main hall.

The main living room incorporated her love of distressed and painted country French furniture combined with modern, straight-lined functional pieces and a bevy of carved and painted decoys. The furnishings were covered in natural-colored and lightly patterned linen, with plump down cushions. The walls were dotted with works by favored artists Madeline Hewes and Mary Faulconer, along with a pair of watercolors of great friend Jackie Onassis by artist Lily Emmet Cushing. Tabletops were scattered with topiary standards, pottery jugs full of fresh flowers from the garden, and shells from walks along the beach, as well as books, magazines and sentimental trinkets of nautical origin.

Mr. Mellon's upstairs bedroom was outfitted like the interior of a cabin on a ship. His three-quarter-sized bed was inset into an alcove in the wall, allowing maximum usage of space. (It is interesting to note that a billionaire could live in such a modestly proportioned and spartan space. There was no room for grandiosity in the Mellon household.) He had a desk and a comfortable chair and windows with views that stretched across the Nantucket Sound. The walls were populated with small paintings and personal artifacts such as little drawings by Bunny.

The property, which included a cottage called the Dune House, an art studio, a greenhouse and service buildings, was protected by cameras discreetly hidden in weathered birdhouses. Grandson Thomas Lloyd remembers that Bunny "especially loved the Dune House" and its "collection of small rooms that open out one to the other with simple understatement," making it "the place where my grandparents often would retreat when the ebb and flow of the summer season became too much."

Another hideout that now holds a place in American presidential lore was the Beach House, which Bunny described as "a small fisherman-like house built into a dune on the Sepuit River," which she added, wasn't "really a river, but a wide band of water that flows between the mainland and a thin strip of sand." A short walk from the Main House, it was fronted with a sheltered deck charmingly furnished with wicker chairs and potted plants, and there was a large wood-burning fireplace that brought warmth and comfort on chilly Cape days. An outdoor grill was near the dock where boats could tie up. Bunny and Paul kept cash on hand to buy hot dogs from the "dog boat" that made daily rounds up and down the river.

"It was a summer's day in August 1961. A clear day except where the oceans have melted Cape Cod into the sky. There was laughter and excited conversation coming from the kitchen side of this otherwise tranquil and protected area. We were going to have a picnic" at the Beach House, Bunny remembered, and the guests included President and Mrs. Kennedy, who were sailing over from Hyannis Port to enjoy a seaside repast.

PREVIOUS OVERLEAF: Rear façade of Cape Cod Main house facing the Sepuit River to Dead Neck Island and beyond to Nantucket Sound. The seasonal dock is visible in the foreground. A favorite honey locust tree is seen to the right, nestled next to the house.

ABOVE: Aerial view of the garden with greenhouse on the north side of the property. **BELOW LEFT:** Garden pavilion for storage influenced by George Washington's Mount Vernon. **BELOW RIGHT:** The south side of the rambling shingled structure faces Nantucket Sound.

Preparing for the picnic in the large, commercial-grade Main House kitchen was a team of trusted staff, some of whom traveled with the Mellons from Virginia as supplemental support for the season. As Bunny noted in her journal,

> *They were part of the family. The generation before them had been with my father. David Banks had been the son of our shepherd. He and I were the same age. He had no real education, but he was bright and he missed nothing. He loved his work, learning quietly and well all he was taught. He also understood human nature. He watched over me like a Lion. If the wrong person in his estimation came too often to the house, he would mumble as he passed by me—"'T ain't no fit company for you, miss. No indeedy—'T ain't right." Nine times out of ten he was right.*

There was a rhythm to those summer days, according to Linda Evora, who worked as a chambermaid and laundress from 1999 to 2009, beginning just two months before Paul Mellon's death. "Mrs. Mellon was so nice, and she respected and valued her employees," Linda commented. At 9:00 a.m. the first tray, a breakfast "starter tray," was taken upstairs to Mrs. Mellon in her bedroom, which Linda described as "Bunny's haven, a combination office, art studio—everything was in her bedroom." The starter included a half of pink grapefruit, cereal, and on the side was a glass of milk for the cereal, a spoonful of sugar for the grapefruit, which was sliced apart and served in the grapefruit half, and a glass of orange juice. At 9:30, the breakfast tray was removed and Bunny gave her request for breakfast, which was served at 10:00. A typical breakfast included fried green tomato, bacala, rice, boiled egg, parsley, one slice of bacon and a cup of coffee with the cream stirred in. Sometimes chipped beef was served.

After breakfast, Bunny went for a swim alone, often commenting afterward how much she loved the water and how good it made her feel. The staff didn't think she should swim alone. An employee kept a watchful eye on Bunny from an undetected position in the art studio, a small building within sight of the water. An employee lunch was served daily at 11:00 a.m. Bunny ate lunch by herself every day at 1:30, either in her bedroom or the living room. Sometimes, if there was company, lunch would be served at the Dune House next door. The afternoons were spent arranging garden flowers, walking, reading, crocheting and relaxing. She enjoyed being alone and wasn't much for company. She mostly dressed casually in pants and a T-shirt, with sandals or sneakers. And she didn't care a smidge about her hair, even though there was a professional salon located in the house.

ABOVE LEFT: The beach picnic house, situated by the Sepuit River. **ABOVE RIGHT:** Jackie Kennedy enjoys the quiet restraint provided by Bunny and Paul at the beach house. **BELOW LEFT:** Cozy wicker chair buffeted from the strong breeze. **BELOW RIGHT:** Bunny's love of gingham cloths echoes from her time as a child with Grandpa Lowe; here a typical picnic lunch buffet is set out.

FAR LEFT: A Eugène Boudin painting above the fireplace with its carved wood relief. Her mantels typically held an assortment of sentimental objects and pictures, eschewing a more formal arrangement. Chair in foreground may be found in many iterations throughout Bunny's houses; detail. **ABOVE:** Living room overlooking the water, with punches of Bunny blue in an otherwise neutral palette. Inviting soft cushions, loose slipcovers, woven rattan chairs, low painted tables laden with books and magazines, and her myrtle topiaries created a light-filled space that did not compete with the views. **BELOW:** A few of Bunny's favorite things in a living room detail: her straw hat with ribbon, a topiary, and a corner with her favorite Billy Baldwin uplighting.

Dinner was served in the dining room, but during later years, it was served on trays in her bedroom or the living room—or sometimes in the dining room, where the sweeping views looked toward Nantucket Sound.

Scattered around the house, small ink and Listerine bottles held flower stems, wooden boat models were on display, and tables and desks were often turned perpendicular to a window, providing seating with a view for two—for supper or desk work.

Bunny's style sensibility extended to the out-of-doors at the Cape, mingling form with function. Jay MacMullan, president of Mainstay Landscaping in Osterville, Massachusetts, who manages the gardens and grounds of the Mellon Cape Cod estates, explained to me in an on-site interview that during Bunny Mellon's occupancy, hand tools and handmade wooden barrels were kept at-the-ready (never a power tool). Seasoned firewood was stacked and stowed in garden sheds painted with faux-weathered exteriors that had been architecturally inspired by at least two works of art by one of Paul Mellon's favorite artists, George Stubbs—*Hambletonian, Rubbing Down* (1799) and *Gimcrack with John Pratt up on Newmarket Heath* (1765). The shed design, explained MacMullan, is also unique in that it provides for an orderly access to storage on all four sides.

MacMullan expertly restored Bunny's Cape Cod gardens through careful cultivation of the soil, allowing dormant seeds to spring to new life, including *Verbena bonariensis*, one of Bunny's favorite summer flowers. The gardens surrounding the compound were originally excavated six to eight feet below the surface and filled with the choicest Barnstable County farm soil, creating a soil "rooted in rich loam instead of saltwater sand," MacMullan said.

Putnam House, a large yellow historic clapboard colonial house purchased by the Mellons and upfitted for modern-day family life for Bunny's son, Tuffy, his wife, Anne, and their two sons remains in the family as of this writing. It connects by shoreline to the main Osterville property and shares the same views of Nantucket Sound.

PREVIOUS OVERLEAF: Dining room ready for lunch, presided over by a Raoul Dufy painting. The trestle table, from her father's ship, is now in the Mystic Seaport Museum in Connecticut. Breakfast table and chair on the right sit in the window overlooking the stone and grass terrace and out to the water. **FACING:** A hooked rug runner leads upstairs from the lower living room, **ABOVE,** to the children's guest wing. Structured like Oak Spring, the Cape Cod house had separate sections that gave privacy to Bunny and Paul and to their children and guests.

FACING ABOVE: A watercolor by frequent and intimate Mellon summer guest John Baskett of his bedroom. **FACING BELOW:** Details of bedside table in Bunny's bedroom. She preferred loose single stems of flowers in small vases to create her own interior garden. **ABOVE:** With her customary shutters thrown open to let light flood in, Bunny's desk is laden with baskets of papers and to-do lists. The fireplace and angled ceiling add to the cozy qualities she enjoyed in her rooms.

FACING ABOVE LEFT: Bunny curls up with a favorite friend for an afternoon nap in the living room, a painted butterfly table resting in front of the sofa. FACING TOP RIGHT: After fifty years of marriage, Paul and Bunny Mellon continued to rely on the strength and support of each other. FACING BELOW: Another view of the living room in the early years. Paintings often found new homes as the Mellons' collection grew. RIGHT: A corner of the living room where carved and painted whistling swan and duck decoys nestle beneath a table.

FACING ABOVE: Cape Cod Dune House porch. **FACING BELOW LEFT:** A quiet side porch. **FACING BELOW RIGHT:** Bunny on the seasonal dock looking out to Nantucket Sound. **ABOVE:** Garden pavilion in the Dune House walled garden. **RIGHT ABOVE:** Blossoms spring forth from crevices, creating a natural, non-structured feeling. **RIGHT MIDDLE:** Bunny relaxes with a friend in the beach picnic house by the Sepuit River. **BELOW:** Daisies in profusion encroach upon tennis court.

LEFT: When Bunny and Paul built the Dune House, they added the pool, which is situated right on the water. At the time, there were no worries of restrictions such as fences. In true Bunny style, the terrace overlooking the pool embodies her love of flowers blooming freely in the cracks, in this case alyssum. **ABOVE:** Side view of Dune House with door open to Bunny's suite.

OVERLEAF LEFT, ABOVE LEFT: Desk overlooking Dune House walled garden, where close friend Jackie Kennedy Onassis spent time drawing and painting. **ABOVE RIGHT:** Cozy seating group by fireplace of Dune House living room. **BELOW:** View across Dune House living room to slipcovered sofa, Georges Braque *Birds* hanging above. **OVERLEAF RIGHT:** Fireplace end of Dune House living room.

FACING ABOVE: Bunny's Dune House bath, replete with fireplace, fabric-covered walls, French side chair, and a small "Bunny table" holding a Porthault towel. Interestingly, Bunny preferred soft, neutral, Berber carpeting in many of her baths. **FACING BELOW:** Bunny's bedroom possesses many of her staples of style: a canopy bed, small fireplace, overstuffed chaise, wicker, a simple "sawhorse" table used as a desk, and, of course, a topiary.

ABOVE: Dune House guest room corner. The fireplace with its customary wicker basket of kindling and soot brush sits between windows that employ Bunny's special shutters, split near the top for privacy yet allowing in light. To the left is one of her TV trays found throughout her homes. They were fabricated in her workshop and were then painted and striéd or crosshatched.

FACING: Putnam House. Bunny and Paul acquired this property and historic home, which shared the boundary and coastline of the other Cape properties. It was for the use of her son, Stacy Lloyd III, and his wife, Anne, and their children. **THIS PAGE:** Various snippets from the Putnam House guest house, the "Barn," which has two separate wings. **OVERLEAF:** Furnishings, art, and views from Putnam House. The central painting on the left page is Bunny as painted by artist Charles Baskerville.

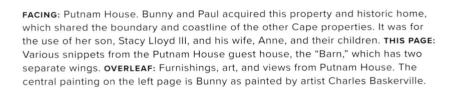

NANTUCKET HOUSE

THE IDEA OF HAVING A HOUSE ON AN ISLAND was most likely instilled in Bunny by Grandpa Lowe from a very young age. He wrote in 1912 from Aspinwall Island, Sharbot Lake, Ontario, Canada:

> *My dearest Bunny: When you receive this letter you will be two years old—a big girl. I hope you will have a pleasant birthday and I wish that we could see you on that day. You will spend it with Mother and Daddy. Grandma and Grandpa are on a most beautiful Island and Bunny would love it here. We feed the birds all the time with crumbs of bread, we put cherries out and the robins came and ate them all. Papa has gone fishing for salmon this morning. He fishes all the time and likes it. Do you go to the ocean every day? . . . I did enjoy going over to the ocean with you and mother. And it is a pleasant memory.*

Gerard Lambert "gave Lily, Gerard and me each a million dollars," Bunny wrote, describing the inheritance from her father. Even though she lived in "a world of great wealth," as the wife of Paul Mellon she was "free" and felt "like a shiny polished penny that is not encumbered with the weight that great wealth brings." With this inheritance Bunny sought a place where she could enjoy solitude and the luxury of privacy, choosing a remote location on Nantucket Island.

"My grandmother was a very private individual who liked being alone," Thomas Lloyd confided, "and she didn't like to socialize."

Herman Melville described Nantucket in his great volume *Moby Dick*, writing that "there was a fine, boisterous something about everything connected with that famous old island." Virginia Scott Heard wrote in *Nantucket Gardens and Houses* that "Nantucket is a microcosm of architectural, interior, and garden styles—one of the most eclectic places on earth." Bunny's friend Daniel Sutherland said the property "looks like a Winslow Homer landscape painting."

In the beginning, Bunny would fly with Jackie Kennedy from the Cape to her Nantucket property, where they would spread a blanket on a bluff high above the

In a 1982 handwritten note to Abbie Zabar, an artist and Nantucket homeowner, Bunny wrote, in part, "I look forward to the day I can build a small house on my land by the sea." The Nantucket estate was sited on 210 acres in Forked Pond Valley, on the island's southern shore. The house, which was relocated from its original site near the eroding shoreline, was reached by traveling across the moors on an unpaved track, repositioned by Mrs. Mellon, which was lined with arrowwood, bayberry, heather, and scrub oak. Bunny never lived here but sometimes stayed overnight.

ABOVE: Views of the island's southern shore in the hazy light of late summer reveal the majestic beauty of Nantucket, which means "faraway island." **FACING ABOVE:** The entrance to the estate, marked with a Braque-styled bird finial and a sign of caution, "Slowly Please Blind Corner Ahead," held views across the meadow to a bluff overlooking

Tom Nevers Head, formerly occupied by the island's old whaling lookout station, to the Atlantic. **BELOW LEFT:** Detail of Bunny's paint technique for giving new wood a weathered look. **BELOW MIDDLE:** When the trees she planted didn't survive, Bunny devised an ingenious method of adaptive reuse, staking out the wooden tree-shaped forms she typically used in determining tree placement, creating the much-desired and sheltering ambiance of trees. **BELOW RIGHT:** The first structure Bunny built on the site was a picnic house. However, the first structure, and then the second, didn't meet Bunny's expectations and were torn down. The third one was the charm.

Atlantic Ocean, share a picnic lunch basket, and dream about the house that Bunny would build. The first structure Bunny built was a small picnic house that mostly provided protection from the elements and shelter from the sun.

"I. M. Pei decided where the main house would be sited," remembered Thomas. Bunny gathered a trusted team to bring her plans to life. It was a complex group of individuals who took exceptional pride in their work and craftsmanship—as well as an effusive pride in working with Bunny Mellon. She surrounded herself with people with differing personality traits. There were creative artisans like Daniel Sutherland who understood her style, best illustrated in the paint techniques he used to achieve her weathered look. As Daniel said, "It had to look old, but not be old." Daniel's expertise in applying the milky glazes to walls added texture and a distressed look without it ever appearing contrived—a natural aging patina. Thomas shared that "there were guys like Bam, a hard-nosed, opinionated, skilled craftsman, Harvard-educated, who had ideas of his own that he shared out loud. He wasn't a yes man, and she liked that."

After a time, and recognizing the damaging effects of beach erosion, Bunny accepted the fact that the house was doomed, and instead of letting it fall into the sea as other islanders had done, she chose to move it inland. It wasn't the first time she had put a house on rollers to relocate it. This time, though, she was moving a house of her own creation—one that had come to life through the blood, sweat and tears of her team. Moving the house was troublesome to her team, because, "it was their house, too," Thomas noted. "It was a painful process because they all had to let things go." For example, in the first house there had been sweeping views of the ocean from Bunny's bedroom—and in the new house, there weren't. Bunny adapted and made the new house work, but Bam, who had poured himself into the fine details, found the situation heartbreaking.

Bunny also cultivated a friendship with Andy Oates, a weaver and the talent behind the one-of-a-kind Nantucket Looms in downtown Nantucket. She wrote in her journal, "A smile in Nantucket from Andy Oates. Our soda together in a messy summer drugstore—wind—salt and sun on our faces and hands." Oates's linen and ramie fabric was considered one of the top ten textiles of the twentieth century. Bunny had such a deep appreciation for his woven textiles that, with Paul's help, she secured mortgage financing enabling Oates and his partner, William Euler, to purchase the building that housed the Looms on Main Street.

Many of those very textiles made their way into Bunny's seaside escape, which "Paul Mellon nicknamed 'Wuthering Heights,'" says Thomas. The New England–style shingled cottage possessed Bunny's spare and unpretentious qualities. Her favorite hues of blue were painted in diamond patterns on the floors. In the entry, the floor was painted with the directional compass coordinates denoting the position of the house. This interior was very humble and personal.

ABOVE: This red, blue, and green Scottish tartan carpet was a nod to the early weavers on Nantucket. In need of the assistance of tradespeople, the early founders of Nantucket gave a half share of ownership to people skilled in the arts of weaving, milling, and building. The only stipulation was that they must live on Nantucket and ply their trade for a period of at least three years.

OVERLEAF LEFT: The tartan was used in varying scales to cover cushions and a bench seat cover. **OVERLEAF RIGHT:** Along with her collection of books on fairy tales and folklore, Bunny also collected whimsical doll-house-sized furniture that could be shifted to serve as bookends.

The bright white interiors with crude antique Shaker cupboards in washed blues were set off by red and blue tartan wool carpets, a departure from the typical Mellon formula. Bunny's love of Scottish tartan blankets inspired the woven carpet.

Built-in bookcases continued the feeling of being on a ship at sea. They were filled with objects and paintings collected from local shops. Bunny always found treasures along the way; they didn't have to be grand and expensive, just appealing to the eye.

Bunny's bedroom featured a wooden canopy bed that looked very modern, with no adornment or fabrication on the canopy. Through the windows behind the bed Bunny said she could stare straight to England. In one of the dormers sat a painted New England chair in a faded floral linen and a table created on the farm; here she would often take her meals. The windows were always open to welcome the sounds and smells of the ocean.

This love of the ocean and its breezes is evident in Bunny's charming picnic house, with its bright white, vertical shiplap walls and painted blue and white floor. Bunny would serve small groups of four or fewer for special, intimate lunches. Guests sat in white director's chairs with blue canvas seats and backs. The table was often covered in one of Bunny's many gingham tablecloths. In the corner stood a special "Bunny bar" for libation and refreshment. Christopher Spitzmiller, whose eponymous company is known for its one-of-a-kind lamps, spent his teenage summers as a salesman at the Osterville House and Garden store. He shared this story with me:

> One day a lady in a crisp white shirt, long denim skirt, and matching denim hat glided in. She towered above me and asked for eighteen folding canvas director's chairs. I looked up at this very distinguished yet understated woman and posed the bewildering question, "Do you really need eighteen of these?" She went on to explain she needed twelve for a table by her pool, four for her garden, and four for a patio elsewhere. I told her that we didn't have that many in stock, but we would be happy to order them. She placed the order and charged the sale to Mrs. Paul Mellon. I went home and relayed what had happened to my grandfather, who knew exactly who Bunny Mellon was. They were both fans of antique wooden boats, and my grandfather knew that she had a whole collection of dories, long wooden rowboats taken from shore and back to larger sail boats.

Surrounding the garden areas of the property were low shingled walls to buffer the winds and protect the flowers. Not satisfied to merely paint these shingles, Bunny employed special formulas for applying layers of paint to create a weathered effect. This painstaking process was evident in most of her residences, from interior walls to furniture to exterior fencing. Once Bunny liked something, she liked it!

ABOVE: Detail of upstairs bedroom. A feeling of serenity fills this space, which has views toward the sea. **ABOVE RIGHT:** A wooden box painted in Nantucket Red, which is a red that has faded to a shade of pink over time and has come to represent a love for the island, complements a table for two. **BELOW:** Bunny's open-canopy bed, Shaker style.

OVERLEAF LEFT: Favorite themes of painted floors, cupboards, and chairs are pictured here with Bunny's preferred method of ceiling lighting, which imparted a soft glow to the room. Bunny admired objects for their function and beauty.

ABOVE LEFT: Bunny enjoyed sailing with her father. A photograph of one of his sailboats is displayed with a collection of sailing paraphernalia. **BELOW RIGHT:** Painted floors such as this compass coordinate, a hallmark of Bunny's interior style, were executed by Paul Leonard, who said he "liked to create settings for something wonderful to happen in." Leonard crafted this effect in the Swedish custom of painting floors to look like marble. Bunny also appreciated the quietness of the wood underfoot.

Bunny's picnic house. John Baskett wrote that "Nantucket held a special place in Bunny's heart, as she had bought the plot and built over it entirely at her own expense with monies that her father had left her." Bunny and Paul "often flew over from Barnstable for the day to do a tour of inspection" and enjoy a picnic.

ANTIGUA ESTATE

LOOKING BACK ON HER FIRST VISIT TO ANTIGUA, Bunny wrote sometime in the late 1980s, "It's been 25 years since we landed in Antigua" looking for "a warm climate beyond the shores of Florida and [the Bahamas.]" At the time, the West Indies island was a remote, quiet and unspoiled place, boasting a landing strip and a beautiful but dry and harsh climate. Recommended by a friend of the Mellons, the island entranced Bunny.

> *It was on this first drive across the island that I became aware of its extraordinary beauty. The road wound through the country as if laid out by animals who knew their way back and forth to water or a sheltering place. On both sides sugar cane blew in the wind, a pale yellow-green, its edges swept the clear blue of the sky. . . . The midday sun was hot. . . . All along our way were the people of the island pursuing their morning tasks.*

Bunny commented on the elegance of the women, with "beads wound around multi-color turbans," whose "style would be the envy of a French lady of fashion. Rarely has anyone ever captured with pencil or brush this elusive gift of charm. I wish they would try."

The new house, whimsically named King's Leap, was designed by Bunny in collaboration with H. Page Cross and built by the local Clarence Johnson Construction Company. Diana Vreeland, editor of *Vogue* magazine, sent staff writer Alison Harwood to scout the Mellons' Antigua home while it was still under construction for a potential feature story. Harwood reported that Mrs. Mellon was "in love, passionately in love with this beautiful creation." Noting that "everything is right," at the conclusion of her lengthy report found among Mrs. Mellon's papers, Harwood summed up the details:

Every room has high tray ceilings, French doors opening onto a court, terrace or lawn and wooden floors over-painted in a pavement pattern . . . faded, worn-looking, charming. The loggia living room has walls painted right over the tray edge to the ceiling in wide stripes of pale gray, apricot, and white—straw chairs painted, deep sofas all in marvelous cotton Tillett's prints. Straight hanging white cotton shades that keep out the sun and let in the breeze can be rolled up and held in place by white tapes tied in neat bows. Mrs. Mellon's bedroom is pale blue and white with a blue and white geometric floor, blue and white printed cotton canopy and spread on a white tester bed with white shutter doors opening to her private terrace garden. Island craftsmen created a writing table with a worn-looking slab of wood that was painted blue and white and supported by metal saw-horse legs. The beds are a slender four-poster frame of white enameled iron, topped by simple brass finials and a tray-ceiling canopy. Each bed's canopy and spread is of a printed cotton to match the room's walls, pale blue and white, yellow and white, etc. Each canopy is edged in heavy white fringe lined with stretched and pleated white cotton. The headboards, quilted pads of the print, bow tufted and tied to the frame with bow-tied tapes. Pulled back from the canopy inside each bed, a cloud of filmy white mosquito netting to release like a sheer cage of night . . . more romantic screened windows. . . .

The pale blue and white dining room is furnished with three round-topped tables painted faux lapis lazuli. The chairs are French country with rush seats. Opening off the dining room is a slat-roofed courtyard garden, paved with coral blocks and surrounded with pots and tubs of trees and plants. The far wall is a row of shelves on which stand a collection of blue and white Chinese cache pots. "Mrs. Mellon is still experimenting with the steeply pitched lath roof to get just the right play of light and shade, accessible to the breezes. This garden room will become part of the dining room."

In the great drawing room, French doors open to a seaward terrace along its opposite wall. Its coloring—pale blues and white—its kick a great painted armoire filled with glorious blue and white Chinese porcelains. "To one side, stereophonic equipment and stacks of records."

Off the narrow loggia, the master bedroom corridor—against its wall a hat rack with "Mrs. Mellon's soft denim cloches in brilliant colors. She always plucks one off before she goes out into the sun." The library is an air-conditioned suite in which Mr. Mellon can work in quiet comfort or an extra guest can be put up. White walls with the "green room" print in lacquer-red papered the wall behind rows of white bookshelves. There was a squashy daybed and a French woven wicker chaise.

PREVIOUS OVERLEAF: One of a series of watercolors by Mossy Fuller, commissioned by Bunny Mellon; detail.

RIGHT: The Mellons' Antigua compound, King's Leap. Amid all the simplicity and restraint of the home, there was very clear intent and comprehensiveness behind the scenes. At the time they built the house, Bunny built the single largest desalinization mechanism on the island, which provided water for the household and the acres and acres of plants in all her gardens. There were also cisterns under the house to catch rainwater from the roof and a huge concrete catch basin down the hill. **BELOW:** The splendid rectangular pool overlooking Half Moon Bay was an anchoring point for the Mellons and their many guests. Unlike her other swimming pools, which she painted deep blue, the Antigua pool was painted light blue, in response to the surrounding landscape.

FACING: Entering from the guest wing, the first room in the main house was the living room, nicknamed by Bunny the "Monkey Room," after her Madeline Hewes painting above the sofa. LEFT: Another room view. BELOW: Detail of a different Madeline Hewes monkey painting.

OVERLEAF: The great drawing room with Paul Leonard's painted floors and Raoul Dufy's *The Regattas at Henley* painting above the sofa. Doors are open toward the courtyard for tropical cross breezes.

LEFT: Detail of *The Regattas at Henley*, 1937, by Raoul Dufy. He was a particularly favorite artist of Paul and Bunny; they had his works present in all their residences. This one now resides at The National Gallery of Art. **ABOVE AND BELOW:** Two untitled works by Madeline Hewes, who became one of Mrs. Mellon's favorite artists, she told her grandson Thomas Lloyd. Bunny commissioned her to do countless paintings of Mellon properties around the world.

Harwood noted that she "saw a large bottle of Erno Laszlo's sun-tan lotion on a table by the pool. It's a pretty rosy color, isn't greasy, smells pleasant and Mrs. Mellon swears by it." And, she closed by saying that "Mrs. Mellon is a darling about giving credit to others . . . to Page Cross for the buildings; to Billy Baldwin for furniture, and more importantly, its arrangement; to the two young set designers who painted the walls and floors, etc." Harwood adored "her total lack of creative ego. . . . She admits mistakes with the candor of the perfectionist, dreams and tries and tries again. . . . Her inventiveness is flourishing and a personal style emerges. I have no doubt but that she really wants you to have this house for *Vogue*, but only when she feels it to be ready."

By the 1980s, Bunny had commissioned local watercolor artist Mossy Fuller to do some paintings for her. Having no "formal training," Fuller wrote that she was "somewhat in awe of doing any work for her as I was well aware of her vast, priceless art collection." However, she put Fuller "quite at ease," discussing the botanical studies and showing her "samples of how she would like them set out." Fuller remembered Bunny as being "quite specific," and that "she hated purple shadows." With her artist's eye, Fuller observed "possible still-life settings all over the place featuring bird cages, baskets, fruit, umbrellas and chairs."

Fuller noted that Bunny "often had house guests, including Jackie Onassis." With sketch pad and paints, and a glass of apple juice brought to her on a tray, Fuller worked on the botanical studies. She shared a story of a large cut-stone wall that had been built near the entrance to the property being "dismantled and moved one foot back from its original place."

The staff was composed of local people, Fuller said, who were "religious and very respectful" and paid little attention to "how well known or wealthy a person was." The staff was dressed in beautifully designed frocks and ensembles designed by Hubert de Givenchy, one for each day of the week. Givenchy with Philippe Venet were frequent guests.

Fuller added delightful details. "The garden was simple but stylish," and due to the dry conditions, Bunny used "whatever plants were available locally and would propagate whenever possible." Grass was substituted with creeping vines and Bunny was "very fond of citrus trees." The black willow was a "favorite amongst indigenous trees" that Bunny "pruned into her chosen shape."

"Bunny runs the houses beautifully," said a frequent guest, who was quoted by the art critic Martin Filler in his article "Cool Mellon" in the April 1992 issue of *Vanity Fair*.

As Edward Klein noted in *Farewell, Jackie*:

> It's the best. Usually, it's a group of four or five [guests] at the most. And you're surrounded by smiling faces who want to do things for you. She's got people who have been there thirty years, and she's always seen that everything is perfect.

FACING: A simple, clean vignette centers on an adapted chest. Slatted doors open onto a porch with sweeping views across Half Moon Bay.

Bunny's grandson Thomas Lloyd remembers visits to King's Leap: "Antigua arguably combined the best elements of my grandmother's style aesthetic and surrounding natural environment. Each room connected openly to another via coral stone walkways, flanked by beautiful paintings opposite lush, pruned gardens. The sounds of tree frogs singing at night paired delightfully with the smell of night-blooming jasmine.

"Breakfast every morning was an incomparable experience. Sitting outside on the terrace facing the ocean with a glass of freshly squeezed orange juice from one of her own orange trees. A tray assembled with a beautiful array of china holding coffee, eggs, bacon, and a separate weave basket of toast. My grandmother's rule was you had to break up at least one piece and feed it to the birds at the table, which the birds were happy to oblige."

In early April 1980, RTCP and JFS [unknown guests] left a hand-written description after their visit to King's Leap, the house that Bunny said she loved the most:

Bunny Mellon, a charming, creative and loving spirit is deeply aware of her friends. Sensing I was weary in body and soul, she performed her special magic by inviting me and a friend to their home in Antigua. I presumed it would be wonderful, because Bunny thought it was. But I was not ready for what awaited.

The winding, narrow, hilly highway with sudden and unexpected turns and wandering sheep and goats took us to the southeastern side of the Island. Finally the road led to stone gateways and long driveways, thick and verdant. The dense growth, the blooming century plants and the tropical atmosphere all added to the mood. When we approached the front of the house, awaiting us was a moment of warmth and joy.

The greeting committee, waiting outside what appeared to be a high-ceilinged cottage, included:

. . . six smiling Antiguan ladies dressed in bright cotton prints with Indian madras turbans on their heads. They were a welcoming party with glowing faces, twinkling eyes and their abundant sense of joy. They laugh and laugh. They are relaxed and warm, gentle and tender and so very human. [The front door led] onto a wide balcony sparsely furnished. There is a large plant here and there and lovely wooden floors. Yet, anything else might go unnoticed. It is here that the balcony becomes a vantage point . . . immersing you in the enchanted, lush beauty that makes this island home a paradise. It is, if you will, a baptism of all your senses.

The collection of rooms in browns, greens, gold and coral, couldn't be seen all at once; "they come later, like presents on Christmas morning," the guests wrote. Empty baskets and water cans "of every shape and size" were spread all around. The Monkey Room, a large living space, was done up in "straw and beige and coral and books," with orange trees in large tubs. Another living room had "smooth wooden floors, painted off-white in a gentle diamond pattern and no rugs. Pale, pale blue walls, slightly textured, white on white and blue." Paintings reflected the surroundings. The sound of the ocean's "pulsating roar, and a constant breeze" could be felt. At night, "white candles flickered inside hurricane lamps and music gently" filled the cool night air. "Chameleons crawl in with hesitancy and finches of every color fly about. Plants seem to grow and rain showers come and go at will, cooling the air, and rainbows sometimes follow."

A wide-angle view of the living room, with French doors to the left opening toward the lush garden pathway to the guest wing, and the corridor on the right aligned perfectly toward Bunny's lime tree garden, facing the ocean.

Billy Baldwin took a great interest in Bunny's Antigua house. In a letter dated September 23, 1980, he wrote:

> *Bunny dear—Ever since we left Antigua I've been thinking about the "big room"— I think the "placement" is so good to look at, and so comfortable. It seems to me that it really "works" now—and will be completed by that one upholstered chair—and a rug. Andy has had the enclosed blue sample made for slip-covers for the sofas and the uphol- stered chairs. I strongly find that the room needs more color and that this blue would be beautiful. Isn't Andy so wonderful to work with? He understands everything instantly! I miss you. It is heavenly here now. Much love, Billy.*

He attached a rough sketch titled "Antigua Drawing Room." He continued his missive:

> *1. Can't the 2 white sofas' slip-covers be copied in Blue if they are sent to New York? And can't the upholstered chair be slip-covered there?—also in Blue? The [Nantucket] Looms will make a sample of the cotton materials, in the medium blue of the Chinese porcelain. It will be a beautiful "background" color for all the existing pillows—and the 2 painted French chairs.*

ABOVE: The opposite side of the living room updated with new wall paint. Wicker chairs and a woven diamond-pattern area rug balance a low center table with a large artwork of fruits by Edme Jean-Baptiste Douet. **FACING:** Tory Burch purchased and updated the property in 2018. Here is the same angle of the living room, with clear changes in patterns and colors but with intentional focus on low tables and chairs, which Bunny loved.

Giving his blessing, he closed by writing, "I see no reason to change anything else—even the Dufy will be benefited." And he signed the letter "Dilatory Domicile."

Baldwin took his friendship with Bunny seriously and seemed to have an uncanny understanding of her.

> *I am so delighted to find now in you, the counts gone—the trust there—the feverish longings cast aside. If this is not true, you have fooled me—perhaps because I want—and pray—to be fooled that way—No—I think that you must be that way to be "practical"—just as you murdered that Black Willow because it was in the way.*

He closed with:

> *Today, I send you real love—In my prayers, I thank God that I know you—and that I have your friendship—I believe that, because mine for you could not flourish if it were one-sided—and flourish it does. Billy.*

FACING: Tory Burch's updated dining room reflects the topiaries and same painted floors that Bunny tailored as her signature style. **ABOVE:** Bunny's dining room, featuring a painted Giacometti chandelier. The hallway leads toward the end of the house and closed doors to Bunny's bedroom.

223

ABOVE: The outside pathway that connected Bunny's bedroom with the great drawing room to the right and dining room behind. The white doors lead into her bedroom. LEFT: This Henri Rousseau painting was moved from room to room over the years. Bunny was known to spontaneously remove a piece of artwork from the wall and relocate it. FACING ABOVE: Lower corridor walkway between the great drawing room and bar held this bench and *Fruits Exotiques*, by Edme Jean-Baptiste Douet. Bunny's art selections for Antigua rooms and hallways open to the exterior held much brown and yellow as balance to the surrounding landscape. FACING BELOW: Painting detail.

Edward Klein in *Farewell, Jackie* wrote, "Jackie's favorite story about Bunny's single-minded devotion to perfectionism concerned how Bunny picked the color for the living room in her house on the grounds of the exclusive Mill Reef Club in Antigua."

> *I was trying to describe to my interior decorator the salmon-pink color that I had in mind. And, I simply told him, "You know how it is when you get up at five o'clock in the mornings, and go into your garden, and the sun is coming up? Well, it's not the color of the light on the first petal of the rose. And it's not the color when you pull off the second petal. It's the color on the third petal. That's what I'm trying to achieve!"*

In *Billy Baldwin: An Autobiography*, written with Michael Gardin, Billy wrote:

> *Their house in Antigua is built of native stone and is completely successful in that it does not look like the rich man's house in the Caribbean. She has accomplished the remarkable feat of creating the most extraordinary gardens there in spite of the difficult circumstance of the lack of water. There is another miracle in that house and that is the food, which is a triumph because it is so delicious. Luckily she had her staff in Virginia to supplement her Caribbean one and she brought some of her beloved servants down there and they taught her staff in Antigua about cooking.*

About twenty years later, and by this time well settled, on March 18, 1980, Bunny wrote, "Back again in this house that becomes more and more part of another century." The day began with Cora, who was "a lovely presence of calm and goodness," who arrived in Bunny's bedroom "ladened with cookbooks we rarely open—and a large menu book." Cora had "learned everything

LEFT: Entrance to the living room from the lawn outside the guest wing. RIGHT: Gardeners were regularly instructed to place food inside the wooden birdhouse for a multitude of tropical visitors. FACING LEFT: A Mossy Fuller painting of the dining room with signature diamond-pattern painted wooden floors, looking out toward the courtyard. FACING RIGHT: Dining room at evening looking inside toward the connecting garden room.

in this house, mostly self-taught with her own sense of taste and love of life and an artistic ability." And the highest compliment, "I love working with her."

After a swim in the sea, breakfast was served on trays. Philippe Venet remembered the trays as a special anecdote of the visit. Grandson Thomas Lloyd also remembers playing Scrabble in the library and seeing his grandmother walk down to the small bar and make a daiquiri.

Bunny wrote, "Arranging flowers is sort of a game here. We bring many things from America that must be juggled around, and little by little our garden is helping." She noted that one of her guests had brought "a lovely dark green faience bowl filled with avocados."

Bunny appreciated the change of seasons: "There is a change in the atmosphere—a different light over the sea. Periwinkle blue. It is spring beginning—everything slowly becomes more sensuous—even the wind."

Bunny's spirit lives on at King's Leap, now the home of Tory Burch and Pierre Yves-Roussel. Initially enthusiasm for the property weighed against concern for restoration. "The bones were all there, but it definitely had a lot of wear and tear," Burch told Hamish Bowles in 2018. Nevertheless, Burch embraced the imperfections Bunny nurtured and her brought-down-from-the-attic look. Burch's architect, Daniel Romualdez, noted, "The layout that Page Cross did is pretty hard to mess with." Other than updating the bathrooms and adding storage in the kitchen, he observed, "We didn't really touch it."

They found the atmosphere beguiling, especially the conservatory, which opened to the dining room, where hummingbirds nested in chandeliers and fluttered over stands of orange trees, tropical plants and palms.

FACING ABOVE LEFT: Slatted-roof greenhouse with pineapple finial sits amid the cutting garden. **FACING ABOVE RIGHT:** A slatted roof covering a small reflecting pool off the guest quarters. **FACING BELOW:** View of courtyard entrance to the main house. The second story leads out to the front path of the house, where guests would be greeted by all the employees upon arrival. **ABOVE:** Romantic view of the coral walkway bench and courtyard between the great drawing room and dining room.

Thomas Lloyd reminisces: "The most indelible aspect of Antigua, fostered by Granbunny, was a place that allowed each family or guest to experience something wholly unique to take with them. Whether it was a quiet moment at the pool feeling the ocean breeze, a retreat into her separate library to read, or a stroll at night down the pathway to the beach, listening to the waves. She allowed you to have your own space and not feel obligated to always be present."

ABOVE: Bunny's bedroom with her ever-present canopy bed, dressed in a Tillett Textiles butterfly fabric; detail. To the left is one of her low tables, created and painted by her workshop for her nighttime reading materials. A lightly painted French caned-back chair pulls up to a writing table. Paul Leonard designed the painted floors in an octagonal pattern. **FACING:** Closeup of writing table.

FACING, CLOCKWISE FROM ABOVE LEFT: Bunny settled in a favorite high-back wicker chair. Paul Mellon in his island study. Hubert de Givenchy at picnic on King's Leap. Bunny and Hubert taking tea on the terrace. CLOCKWISE FROM ABOVE LEFT: Friends share a picnic: Hubert de Givenchy, Billy Baldwin, Phillipe Venet, Bunny. Pouring tea on the terrace. Billy Baldwin works a crossword puzzle. Bunny shops at the local produce market wearing one of her signature hats and ubiquitous Schlumberger enameled bangles. Never one to leave her gardens to others, Bunny worked closely with staff to go over all details of the gardens and grounds.

THE PARIS
APARTMENTS

PAUL MELLON, THE SON OF AN ENGLISHWOMAN, embraced all things English, while his wife Bunny was a Francophile. She had two apartments in Paris—Rue de l' Universite and Avenue Foch, where she later moved in an effort to downsize. John Baskett, the Mellon curator, and his daughter, Samantha, often spent time at Avenue Foch. Samantha Baskett described the experience with what her father called "an almost photographic memory, despite the lapse in time":

> *There were wrought iron gates at the front and you walked into a hall where the floorboards were decorated with diamond shaped squares in distressed blue, gray and ivory. Out of sight, but providing an agreeable smell, were burning pine cones, and there was also lavender. The door on the right led into the living room dominated by a large Rothko painting. Next to it was a painting by Bunny's daughter, Eliza, who was a competent artist. We had dinner in this room seated in armchairs and it was brought in on trays—an arrangement that Bunny chose to do for all of us from time to time.*

A wide staircase with a wrought-iron banister led upstairs, where Paul and Bunny had bedrooms side by side, as they did in all their houses. In Bunny's room, the walls, Samantha wrote,

> *were decorated in fabric with deep blue block-printed flowers on an ivory background. There was a four-poster bed with long windows on either side. Beside the bed was a tiny pot of sweet peas. On the far wall was a little fireplace and above it a small painting by Pissarro of a peasant girl in a deep blue dress (like the fabric on the walls). She was surrounded by emerald green verbiage (the only item in the room that wasn't blue). A little corridor with a built-in cupboard on one side led into the bathroom. There was an enamel bath and above it a shelf of cut glass with bottles containing bath suds.*

Isabelle Rey 95

Paul Mellon often teased Bunny, telling her that their apartment building on Avenue Foch had been occupied by the Gestapo during the war, but, fortunately, John was able to verify that it was not true.

The two apartments possessed many hallmarks of Bunny's style. Paris became a true testing ground for the implementation of many of her signature designs.

Her love of toile de Jouy takes center stage, from wall coverings to canopied bedding to soft furnishings. The floors were, naturally, painted with various colors in geometric patterns. The furniture—diminutive French chairs, iron tables by Giacometti, and comfortable upholstered sofas—along with important works by Rothko, jardinieres of flowers, and baskets of bundled wood by fireplaces guarded by freestanding fire screens of tempered glass created an atmosphere of Bunny's genius mix of "high and low." Her love of all things French included leading design luminaries such as Jean Schlumberger, Cristóbal Balenciaga, and Hubert de Givenchy.

Paris Oct. 23, 1980. Last night Hubert came for dinner. As always the apartment had a wonderful feeling of enchantment. The candles and fire—one window with the shutters open—une tableau dans le jardin—the lights illuminated—the two apple trees filled with yellow fruit. Under one a yellow and a white cat watched her kittens play. The pairing shone after a gentle rain. The borders of herbs. Rosemary, lavender and the last white roses of autumn. The wall reflected the light—the painted beige. . . . The place is becoming too happy. I can not finish this. —Bunny Mellon

PAGE 234: Setting the stage—the entrance hall features a Sophie Grandval cabbage, painted geometric floors, a tôle watering can, and a collection of wicker baskets in this interior watercolor by French artist Isabelle Rey.

PREVIOUS OVERLEAF: A Mark Rothko dominates one end of the airy living room with its mix of Louis XV and Louis XVI fauteuils and carved side chairs.

FACING LEFT: A Louis XVI carved and painted side chair coupled with a modern metal console and antique blue-and-white porcelain create a harmonious blend between old and new. **FACING RIGHT:** A fashion sketch finds a perch in the window. **ABOVE:** Amidst a collection of antique French chairs and Louis XVI ormolu mounted bureau plat, the living room feels chic and spare.

Isabelle Rey 95.

PREVIOUS OVERLEAF: The opposite end of the living with its mix of modern art, flat weave carpet, and modern metal and glass low tables. Watercolor by Isabelle Rey.

FACING: A work by Diebenkorn above the fireplace. **ABOVE LEFT:** A double-tiered modern metal console holds the ingredients for evening refreshment. **ABOVE RIGHT:** A treasured 18th-century Louis XVI brass-mounted mahogany architect's table, which is now housed in Bunny's Oak Spring Garden Library.

THIS PAGE: Bunny shifted furniture from room to room and from apartment to apartment until she found the right spot. The two-tiered metal console seen here is in a different location on page 238. The three photos on the right emphasize this dictum, as chairs and color boards shed light into her design process. **FACING:** The Sophie Grandval cabbage seen on page 234 shows Bunny's ever-changing rotation of art. The bench beneath was frequently used to stack favorite books, while baskets and a topiary rest on the painted floors.

ABOVE: Working on the furniture arrangement and fabric selections. Bunny never discarded, always repurposing furniture for different rooms and apartments. (Note the fauteuil in right foreground and small side chair in front of desk, which were originally used in the dining room, pages 248 and 249). **LEFT:** One of the modern metal and glass fire screens Bunny favored. **FACING:** The bergère (page 246) now has its new covering. The Giacometti "Tree of Life" console has moved from the right of the fireplace to the opposite corner and acts as a bar, replete with the ubiquitous topiary.

ABOVE: Bold wall tiles set the tone for the dining room. The "Tree of Life" console by Giacometti (pages 246 and 247) is seen here in its original location. BELOW: Bunny used uplights (behind the chair) in the corners of her rooms to provide unobtrusive ambient light. FACING: The table with its windowpane check cloth and 18th-century hard-paste porcelain cabbage is ready for luncheon with a set of 18th-century Louis XVI fauteuils.

LEFT: Always a necessity for Bunny was a cozy nook to house her books with a comfortable down-filled chair close by and a small, unobtrusive light or lamp. **FACING:** The stairwell boasts a Giacometti lantern, French wrought-iron railing, and a large French painting.

ABOVE AND FACING ABOVE: Small, cozy fireplaces were a necessity to Bunny. They anchored her rooms with the mantels providing a perfect resting place for a favorite photo, work of art, object, and signature topiary. **FACING BOTTOM LEFT:** A flowering hydrangea painting brings her love of nature and gardening into the room. **FACING BOTTOM RIGHT:** Bunny was always involved in the design process. She is seen here with her toile de Jouy taped to the wall as she inspects the scene.

Bunny's beloved pastoral toile de Jouy fills this bedroom with a soft backdrop for objects, art, and topiaries. **FACING ABOVE LEFT,** A Mary Faulconer painting rests atop a Louis XVI stool. **FACING ABOVE RIGHT:** The door being prepared for its toile covering. **BOTTOM LEFT:** A necessary evil, the television, retreats with its white surround. Bunny used white televisions so as not to have them noticed. **BOTTOM RIGHT:** The *lit à la polonaise* before its transformation. **ABOVE:** The *lit à la polonaise* dressed and ready, with its bright red giving a pop against the blues and whites. Another Bunny "signature" was her ability to achieve scale and balance with extraordinarily small objects like this painting, which works perfectly in the large space.

Bunny's grand *lit à la polonaise*, draped in a Sache of Beauclere fabric, takes center stage between low, whitewashed Giacometti tables and a pair of her topiaries. The Louis XVI bench at the foot of the bed was always full of books and magazines. Note two small paintings above the bed arranged in asymmetrical balance. The spare room has simple off-white curtains and a pair of Louis XVI side chairs in a bright blue hue. Watercolor detail, left, by Isabelle Rey.

FACING AND ABOVE: The *lit à la polonaise* in her earlier Avenue Foch apartment. A bergère chair is swathed in the same fabric, occupying a cozy spot by the fireplace. In her typical manner, a small painting floats well above the mantel. **RIGHT:** Painting detail.

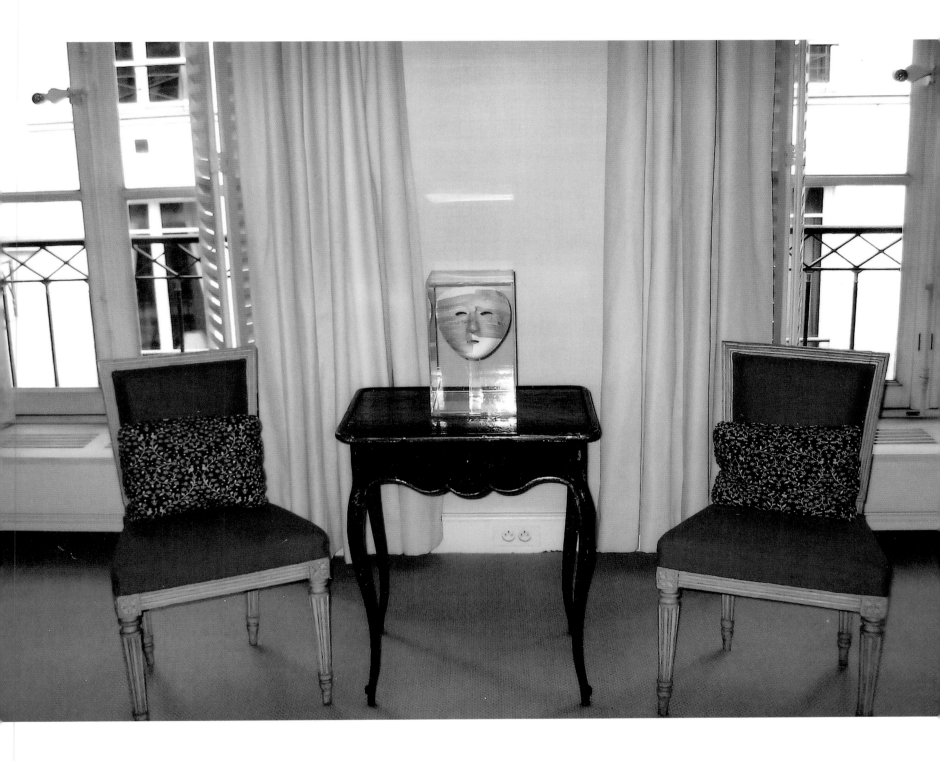

FACING: The same bedroom with a painted and distressed armoire, above which sits part of her collection of woven baskets.
BELOW: Bunny worked out combinations of patterns and colors with her fabrics before deciding which might be the best iteration.
ABOVE: Louis XVI chairs and pillows in various shades of blue reveal Bunny's innate ability to mix many shades of the same color. A favored treasure rests like a modern work of art atop the Louis XV table.

THIS PAGE: Photos of Bunny's daughter, Eliza Lloyd, who found Paris as intoxicating as did her mother. A talented artist, she had an apartment in Paris as well as a studio. ABOVE LEFT: A work in Eliza's studio. BELOW LEFT: Eliza rests on a cushy chaise longue, behind which is one of Bunny's prized birdcages. BELOW RIGHT: Exemplifying the strong bond between mother and daughter. FACING ABOVE LEFT AND RIGHT: Views inside and looking out to the inner courtyard. FACING BELOW LEFT: Whitewashed Giacometti andirons rest inside the fireplace. FACING BELOW RIGHT: Paul Mellon surveys the City of Light. He began collecting French Impressionist art in the 1950s under Bunny's keen eye and influence.

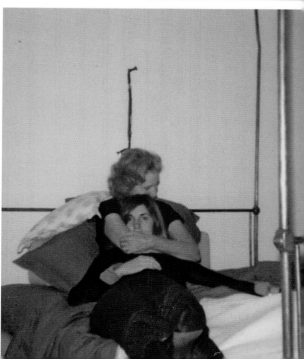

FASHION COLLABORATIONS

A collection of 18-karat gold and paillonné enamel *Dot Losange Bangles*, designed by Jean Schlumberger in 1960. These became Bunny's trademark through the years and she collected them with ardor in every color. Virginia Museum of Fine Arts, Richmond. Collection of Mrs. Paul Mellon.

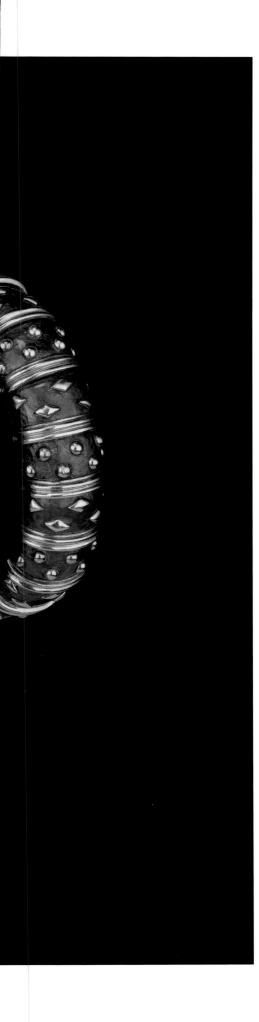

SCHLUMBERGER

BUNNY SOUGHT THE BEST TALENT, WHETHER OR NOT THEY WERE APPRECIATED BY OTHERS. Her focus was on design, and as Baldwin wrote in his autobiography, "There can be no doubt that because of her enthusiasm, support, and appreciation of their talents, that she has helped them on their way."

Bunny's friendship and collaboration with Schlumberger began in 1950 when she visited his salon in Manhattan while she was Christmas shopping. Schlumberger, who Baldwin described as "perhaps the greatest jeweler of our time," believed that, "some women want to look expensive, I would prefer to have them look precious."

And precious they were. His collaborations with Bunny dazzled. Mutually inspired by their appreciation for the things of nature, he created Flower Pot, showcasing a 17-karat blue sapphire called the Dancing Girl of India, a butterfly brooch based on one of Bunny's favorite creatures, which was studded with colored stones and diamonds, and a shell bracelet of diamond, sapphire, and emeralds.

But it was what became known as the Schlumberger bracelet that became ubiquitous to Bunny's wardrobe. "Mrs. Mellon had bracelets in colors of blue, white, green, brown, and a red one studded with diamonds that she wore at Christmas," confided Marie Colandrea, Mrs. Mellon's confidante. Extra bracelets were kept on hand for gift-giving.

One of Bunny's finest collaborations with Schlumberger was a roof finial that was executed in lead by Robert Bradford. It was a bouquet of loosely arranged flowers displayed in an urn that was affixed atop the peak of the central pavilion of the Formal Greenhouse at Oak Spring.

There are all sorts of conjectures about the design of the finial, so let us lay out the truth. As we look back into history, the Kennedy administration won great accolades for the new floral artistry at work in the White House. This artistry was the work of Bunny Mellon; the arrangements were based on her appreciation for fresh garden flowers and old, lovely Dutch still-life paintings. Letitia Baldridge, social secretary to Jacqueline Kennedy, described the floral arrangements at the Kennedy White House in her book *Of Diamonds and Diplomats*, as "delicate small bouquets in vermeil containers, which Mrs. Paul Mellon's gardener taught our White House gardener how to arrange. Exquisitely simple, imitable by any housewife, they were reminiscent of the old, lovely Flemish flower still lifes."

Shells bracelet designed by Schlumberger in 1958 with Bunny's love of the sea as his inspiration. It incorporates sapphires, diamonds, and emeralds set in 18-karat gold. Virginia Museum of Fine Arts, Richmond. Collection of Mrs. Paul Mellon.

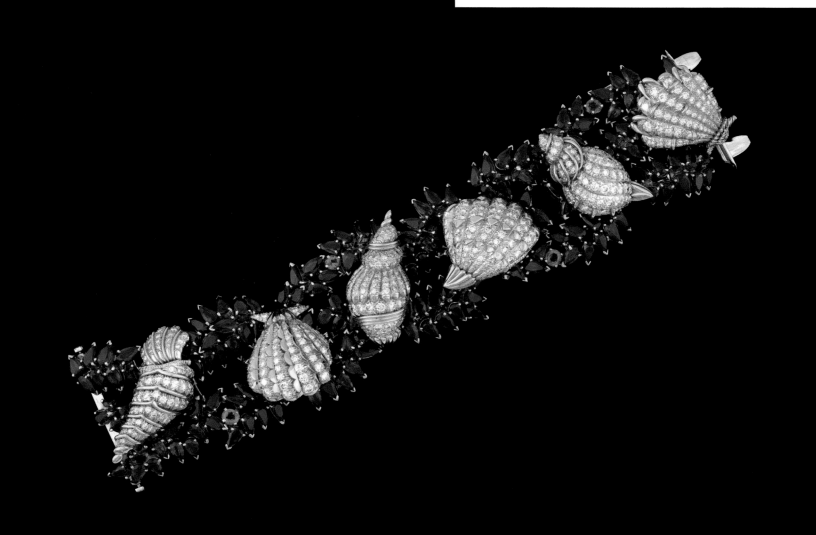

The *Butterflies* bracelet was designed in 1956 by
Schlumberger with Bunny's input and employs hidden
springs to attach the butterflies so they hover above
the flowers and gently "fly." She had two of these,
and they could be joined to form a choker. Virginia
Museum of Fine Arts, Richmond. Collection of Mrs.
Paul Mellon.

FACING LEFT ABOVE: *Study for "Flower Pot": Flower,* ca. 1960, and **BELOW:** *Study for "Flower Pot": Pot Designs,* ca. 1960. Schlumberger sketched various versions of terra-cotta pots from Bunny's greenhouse with different applications of gold and jewels before selecting the simple basket weave in 18-karat gold. Virginia Museum of Fine Arts, Richmond. Gift of the Estate of Jean Schlumberger.

FACING RIGHT: *Flower Pot (Pot de fleurs)* comes to fruition, 1960. It originally featured a rare Kashmir sapphire, which was later replaced with this massive amethyst as the center of a gold flower planted in a terra-cotta pot. It had a detachable diamond clip mounting so the stone could be removed and worn as a brooch. This piece perfectly expressed the creative collaboration between Bunny and Schlumberger. It encompasses the yin and yang of Bunny's style, her brilliant ability to mix the humble with the grand. Virginia Museum of Fine Arts, Richmond. Collection of Mrs. Paul Mellon.

FACING BELOW RIGHT AND BELOW: Schlumberger *Dahlia Hidden-Watch,* 1958, created with 18-karat gold, diamonds, and citrines. Virginia Museum of Fine Arts, Richmond. Collection of Mrs. Paul Mellon.

RIGHT: *Table Clock,* ca. 1962, is 9½ inches tall and is comprised of 18-karat gold and lapis lazuli. Virginia Museum of Fine Arts, Richmond. Collection of Mrs. Paul Mellon.

ABOVE: *Jasmine* necklace, nicknamed "Breath of Spring," has diamond flowers that wind around the 16 colored sapphires in a pattern that appears as if they had actually "grown." Schlumberger is quoted as having said, "I wanted to capture the irregularity of the universe. . . . I observe nature and find verve." Bunny Mellon wore the necklace once in public, to a dinner at the National Gallery of Art marking the retirement of Paul Mellon as chairman of the board. **FACING ABOVE LEFT:** *Leaves (Necklace)* 1956, of turquoise, diamonds, 18-karat gold, and platinum. **FACING ABOVE RIGHT:** *Flowers and Leaves* necklace, c. 1958, of 18-karat gold, platinum, and diamonds.

FACING BELOW LEFT: Two *Torsades* bracelets, c. 1958. The one above is comprised of diamonds, 18-karat gold, and gold beads. The one below, without clasp, consists of coral beads. **FACING BELOW RIGHT:** *Necklace*, late 1950s, of cultured pearls, fancy colored diamond, and sapphires.

All pieces are by Jean Schlumberger (French, 1907–1987). Virginia Museum of Fine Arts, Richmond. Collection of Mrs. Paul Mellon.

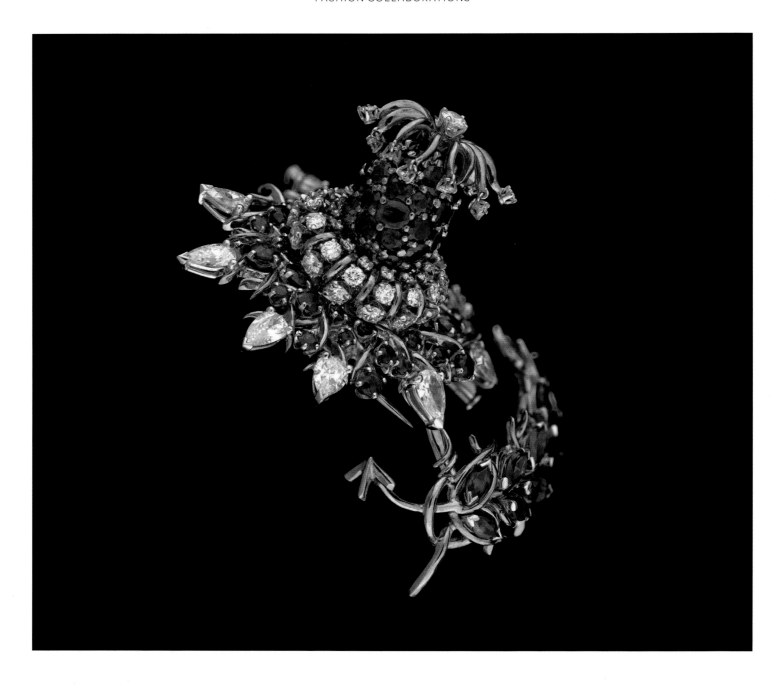

ABOVE: *Flower with Detachable Leaf*, 1964, Jean Schlumberger, comprised of 18-karat gold, platinum, diamonds, and sapphires. Virginia Museum of Fine Arts, Richmond. Collection of Mrs. Paul Mellon.

FACING ABOVE LEFT: *Cruciform Pendant*, early 1970s made of 18-karat gold, platinum, rubies, and diamond. **FACING ABOVE RIGHT:** *Ear Clips*, 1960s, of 18-karat gold, lapis lazuli, diamonds, and cultured pearls. **FACING BELOW LEFT:** *Sea Star*, 1960, with rubies and diamonds set in platinum and 18-karat gold. **FACING BELOW RIGHT:** *Bleuet* brooch, c. 1957, with a 25-carat cushion-cut purple sapphire surrounded with sapphires and diamonds, set in 18-karat gold. All by Jean Schlumberger. Virginia Museum of Fine Arts, Richmond. Collection of Mrs. Paul Mellon.

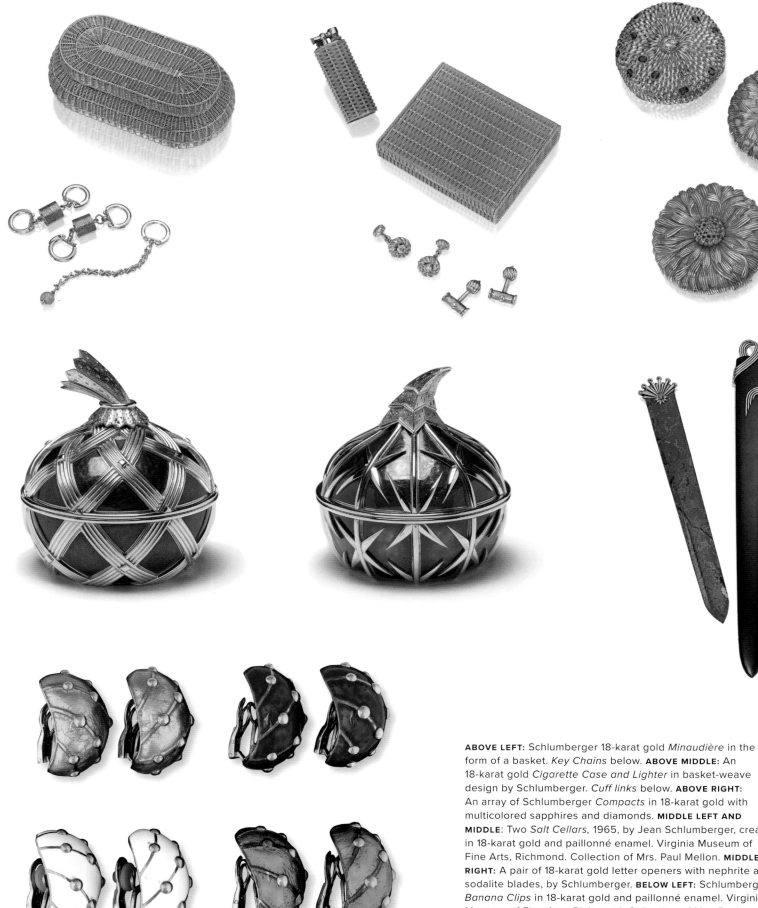

ABOVE LEFT: Schlumberger 18-karat gold *Minaudière* in the form of a basket. *Key Chains* below. **ABOVE MIDDLE:** An 18-karat gold *Cigarette Case and Lighter* in basket-weave design by Schlumberger. *Cuff links* below. **ABOVE RIGHT:** An array of Schlumberger *Compacts* in 18-karat gold with multicolored sapphires and diamonds. **MIDDLE LEFT AND MIDDLE:** Two *Salt Cellars,* 1965, by Jean Schlumberger, created in 18-karat gold and paillonné enamel. Virginia Museum of Fine Arts, Richmond. Collection of Mrs. Paul Mellon. **MIDDLE RIGHT:** A pair of 18-karat gold letter openers with nephrite and sodalite blades, by Schlumberger. **BELOW LEFT:** Schlumberger *Banana Clips* in 18-karat gold and paillonné enamel. Virginia Museum of Fine Arts, Richmond. Collection of Mrs. Paul Mellon.

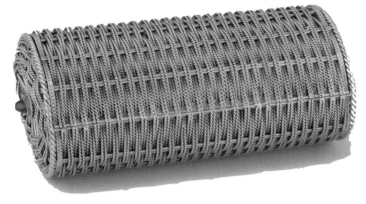

ABOVE LEFT: *Basket-Weave Case with Flowers* (minaudière), c. 1965, by Schlumberger. Comprised of 18-karat two-color gold, diamonds, and enamel. **ABOVE RIGHT:** *Basket-Weave Case* (minaudière), 1959, by Schlumberger, 18-karat gold. Both Virginia Museum of Fine Arts, Richmond. Collection of Mrs. Paul Mellon.

BELOW LEFT: Three fabric and gold handbags by Jean Schlumberger for Christian Dior. **BELOW RIGHT:** Handbag of alligator leather with a spiraled gold wreath clasp by Jean Schlumberger for Christian Dior.

BALENCIAGA

FLOWERS WERE IMPORTANT TO BUNNY, BUT NOT SO MUCH CLOTHES. She said so herself. Even today, if you speak to a local Upperville or Middleburg resident, someone who knew Bunny, they will hesitantly admit that her clothes were "awful." According to Bunny Mellon, Jean Schlumberger wasn't impressed with her wardrobe either and whisked her off to Paris where he introduced her to Cristóbal Balenciaga, the Spanish master tailor and great couturier. Bunny journaled,

> *For more than ten years Balenciaga designed almost my entire wardrobe. . . . From elegant deshabilles to nightdresses or fine batiste petticoats. . . . He perfectly understood that what I needed was both simple working clothes, suitable for the garden or for any other country chores, and extraordinary dresses, coats and hats for dances and soirees.*

Balenciaga transformed her look with what Philippe Venet, a master tailor who had apprenticed at Pierre Court in Lyons, described as "Balenciaga's basic rules": an emphasis on comfort with an expert command of technique and an extraordinary knowledge of fabrics, resulting in creations that made Bunny feel pretty. She carefully compiled the sketches sent to her from Balenciaga into an album she titled *I Feel Pretty.*

Bunny and Jackie Kennedy, also a Balenciaga client, could always pick up their friendship where they left off and did so on April 8, 1968. "Walking into Kenneth's on 54th Street, I found Jackie sitting in a corner of the entrance hall," Bunny wrote. "'Hi,' she said in her quiet voice. 'Have you got a minute? I have a problem.'" The funeral for Martin Luther King, Jr., was being held the next day. Jackie wanted to attend the funeral to pay her respects and offer sympathy "because Mrs. King is now a widow like me."

The next morning, Bunny, dressed in a Balenciaga navy blue wool serge coat with a navy blue velvet beret, departed for Atlanta with Jackie in the Mellons' plane, with "two large baskets, one marked breakfast, the other lunch." They arrived in Atlanta at 8:00 a.m. and "drove to Mrs. King's house," and were led to Mrs. King's bedroom, where a child was jumping on a "huge red and gold bed. Mrs. King, who was dressing for the funeral, was delighted to see Jackie, who with her quiet, strong presence comforted her with understanding and warmth," Bunny wrote. The meeting didn't

last long and they were soon on their way to Ebenezer Baptist Church for the funeral service. Bunny wrote thirty-five years after the event that:

> *My greatest memory is the music. Few instruments, just voices numbering a hundred or more. The voices seemed to come from distant lands, from seas, deserts, plains, lakes and mountains. It overwhelmed the emotions of the congregation, and when the last voice was heard and prayers read, people began to move toward the doors.*

Mrs. Kennedy and Mrs. Mellon were soon back on the plane, where "we untied our big basket."

ABOVE: Balenciaga prized his relationship with Bunny and collaborated with her, as illustrated in *I Feel Pretty*, an album she created with the sketches collected from 1959 to 1962 of the models she selected for purchase. From the moment Bunny selected a model, she was given the option of having it made in different fabrics.

FACING ABOVE LEFT: A day dress in printed piqué. Photo by Paredes. **ABOVE MIDDLE:** A navy blue wool serge coat with a panel of four pleats at the back and a navy blue velvet beret, worn by Bunny Mellon when she accompanied Jacqueline Kennedy to the funeral of the Rev. Martin Luther King, Jr. Photo by Paredes. **ABOVE RIGHT:** Loose garden tunic with diamond-shaped patch pockets in pistachio green cotton taffeta, shown here with her trademark blue bucket hat, an example of the chic working attire Bunny preferred. Photo by Paredes. **BELOW LEFT:** Cool wool taffeta suit in printed white with an abstract black linear pattern. Photo by Paredes. **BELOW MIDDLE:** Quadrille tailored suit in navy blue, one of Bunny's favorite colors. She had a fine appreciation for the craftsmanship of this perfectly tailored masterpiece. The encircling yoke and quadrille fabric are evidence of perfection and knowledge of the trade. Photo by Outumuro. **BELOW RIGHT:** A favored simplified silhouette; the curves of the "cocoon" demonstrate Balenciaga's modern outlook. The expert folds placed at the back of the coat provided ease of movement, allowing air to circulate. Bunny appreciated that the coat was reversible and purchased three versions of it. Photo by Outumuro. **OVERLEAF LEFT:** An evening ensemble featuring an empire line dress and puffed short cape in royal blue silk marquisette, a lightweight open fabric of leno weave, where two warped yarns are twisted around the weft yarns, a technique used to strengthen delicate fabric. Photo by Outumuro. **OVERLEAF RIGHT:** Evening gown in pink faille covered with pink tulle embroidered with multicolored floral motifs. Photo by Paredes.

GIVENCHY

WHEN BALENCIAGA PASSED AWAY SUDDENLY IN 1972, the bonds of Bunny's and Hubert's friendship were strengthened. Attempting to console Givenchy and "take his mind on a new and different path," Bunny suggested that they "go outside and redesign his landscape and gardens that badly need doing." And, with "the help of God, cold air and Hubert's natural creative spirit, there came a small positive response." Bunny recorded in her journal, "Ever since we have been each other's clients—he takes care of the clothes and I take care of the gardens."

Hubert de Givenchy became Bunny's huckleberry friend when Balenciaga closed his Maison de Couture in 1968, and escorted Bunny across the street and introduced her to his mentee, Hubert de Givenchy, explaining her preference to work with one couturier with whom she could "communicate and enjoy the confidence of working together." An "easy and attractive friendship" between Bunny and Hubert "soon followed. He has an extraordinary sense of color, a quick interpretation of ideas and always added his own unique flair and charm," she wrote.

Philippe Venet, Givenchy's partner in business and in life, wrote to me:

> *The Givenchy style is elegant, timeless, classic by day, dazzling at night with a single concern: to enhance a figure and develop the personality of women who wanted to confide in him. Hubert often created new lines without wanting to be fashionable, and as Cristóbal Balenciaga said, "Wanting to be fashionable is already old-fashioned." There was no easy effect. It wasn't supposed to be a costume. You had to see the person before the dress.*

Bunny "liked simple but great quality things. She thought the Givenchy style was exactly what suited her (if it was fur, she wore it as a pelisse in a raincoat). On the other hand, the evening gowns were spectacular and enhanced his wonderful jewelry for the big nights at the National Gallery of Art," Philippe remembered.

Bunny and Hubert shared a love of family tradition. In 2015, M. Givenchy shared with me that during Bunny's fittings, they would talk about art, gardening, houses and family. He, too, was blessed with, and influenced by, an extraordinary grandfather. Only two years old when his father passed away, his maternal grandfather, Jules Badin, became an important influence in his grandson's future career and becoming the preeminent French couturier of the twentieth century. Badin, a student of Corot, "ran the Gobelins and Beauvais tapestry workshops," stated Christiane de Nicolay-Mazery in *Cristóbal Balenciaga, Philippe Venet, Hubert de*

ABOVE LEFT: Photo shared by Philippe Venet of the guest room at Jonchet where Bunny stayed when visiting him and Givenchy. **ABOVE RIGHT:** Sache of Beauclere fabric and a natural jute rug reflect Givenchy and Bunny's shared ideal of an atmosphere devoid of excessive formal elements that embraces beauty, refinement, comfort and coziness. **FACING:** Givenchy wrote in the exhibition catalog for the *Rachel Mellon Collection*, an exhibition he curated, that "Mrs. Paul Mellon was a fine-looking woman, tall, with a dazzling smile and a truly beautiful face. Her style and exceptional refinement were a perfect match for the garments she would choose at Mr. Balenciaga's fashion houses." Bunny "would select her outfits with discernment, showing a strong predilection for navy blue. She had her own enormously comfortable and practical style." Photograph by Joshua Greene, © 2021, detail.

OVERLEAF LEFT, ABOVE AND BELOW LEFT, AND BELOW RIGHT: Bunny sent Givenchy her own hand drawings to illustrate what she wanted. Their mutual affection is revealed in charming expressions of love and her floral sketches. **ABOVE RIGHT:** Bunny, in her trademark navy blue, with her huckleberry friend, Hubert de Givenchy; detail. **OVERLEAF RIGHT: ABOVE LEFT AND RIGHT:** Lively and spirited couture sketches drawn by Givenchy for his friend and client. **BELOW LEFT AND RIGHT:** From Bunny's couture archives, necessary paperwork that documents the creative process, the give and take, between the two collaborators; details.

Givenchy: Grand Traditions of French Couture. "My grandfather's taste is ingrained in me," Givenchy wrote, and "instilled in me my taste for beautiful objects."

World-class landscape designer Madison Cox shared a story about receiving a call from his client Hubert de Givenchy, who had an apartment with a terrace in the Essex Building in New York City. It was July, and Givenchy was planning ahead for a special guest in September. Cox was asked to suggest a plan for a garden for the terrace. It was a small terrace, and there was one tree—dead—in a large tub. Cox suggested that Givenchy purchase a timed watering gadget that could be attached to the hose bibb and would solve the problem. Givenchy approved the hose bibb, but added a clever request: he wanted Cox to plant an apple tree in the planter, and the tree was to bear shiny red apples in September. His friend liked apples, and New York City is known as the Big Apple. This was a rather tricky proposition for an apartment terrace in New York City. Cox soon learned that the special guest was Bunny Mellon and commented on what an extraordinary act of kindness that had been—from one friend for another.

In later years, Givenchy encouraged Bunny by telling her during a late-night phone call, "It's never too late to be chic. . . . Pick yourself up, and let's get back to work. Take what is comfortable and we will make it work."

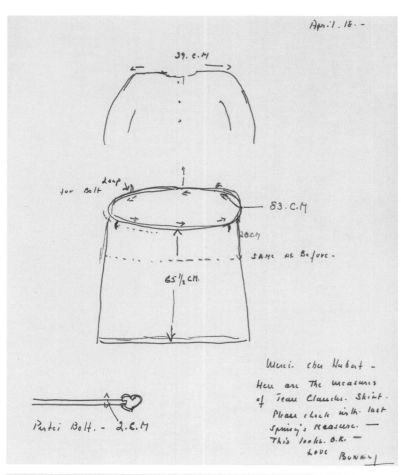

April. 15. —

39. C.M

for Belt loop

83. C.M

20.C.M

SAME AS Before.

65½ CM.

Pintri Belt. — 2. C.M

Merci. cher Hubert —
Here are The measures
of Jean Claudes. Skirt.
Please check with last
spring's Measure. —
This looks. O.K. —
Love BUNNY

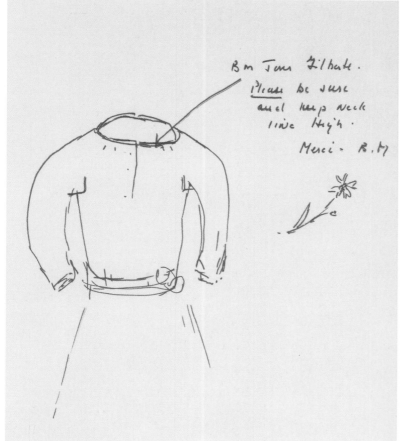

Bon Jour Gilbert.
Please be sure
and keep Neck
line High.
Merci — B. M

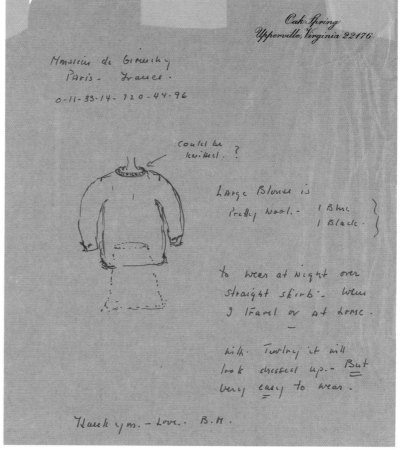

Oak Spring
Upperville, Virginia 22176

Monsieur de Givenchy
PARis — France.
0-11-33-14-720-44-96

Could be
knitted?

LArge Blouse is
Pretty Wool. — 1 Blue
1 Black.

to wear at Night over
straight skirt. — When
I Travel or At home.
—
with. Tweed it will
look dressed up. — But
very easy to wear.

Thank you. — Love.. B. M.

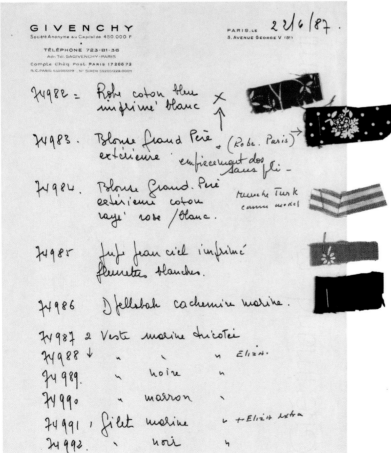

IN CONCLUSION

BUNNY MELLON WAS DRAWN TO BEAUTY AT AN EARLY AGE and throughout her lifetime sought to pair her eager and willing spirit and desire to learn with academic knowledge, hands-on learning, and a willingness to try new things. A designer at heart who always looked for inspiration in her own work, Bunny wrote that it was important "to have an atmosphere that inspires and one can relate to. There must always be a feeling people can take home, even copy or remember later with a positive and thoughtful recall." This applied to every structure that had been graced by her gentle touch, including the church she had designed and supervised the building of in nearby Upperville.

In 2010, the 50th Anniversary and Homecoming of Trinity Episcopal Church was held to celebrate "the first service in the newly constructed church." In preparation for the event, church members and Upperville residents Gray and Anne Coyner, who jointly chaired the event, met with Mrs. Mellon to discuss the particulars of the celebration and to review archival material for a proposed exhibition. The day before the celebration, Bunny went to the church to view the exhibition. Gray Coyner wrote about that visit in an email to me.

> She arrived through the back door to Cox Hall, wearing a beret and her hair skewed under it. I immediately sensed she felt among "old friends" as she toured the display. When she removed her beret, her hair sprang out in all directions, and as I pointed out the plaster models, she asked me where was her unicorn? [in reference to the plaster models carved by Heinz Warneke for the capitals of the columns in the church on display, each depicting various animals of religious significance.] Once I showed it to her, she seemed so comfortable that she proceeded to hug each volunteer as I introduced them to her. She looked at the various drawings, plans, photos, and objects carefully and seemed delighted that all these items were being seen by a new generation of Trinity members. After a few more questions and many thank-yous from both sides, she left as quietly and unobtrusively as she had arrived. Nearly forgetting her beret, she sent her driver back to retrieve it. All the volunteers were so excited to have met her and felt their time was worth every minute for that experience.

On the following Sunday, a sermon was delivered by then Rector Robert Banse, and to help his parishioners better understand all that had gone into the building of the church, he quoted from the first sermon that Robert Cox, the rector at that time, delivered at Trinity. In his sermon Cox shared the sentiments of the artisans he had come to know, who had built the church. Cox said in his sermon:

Perhaps I can best say what I mean by telling two or three stories. One day a famous sculptor spent a long time in this church examining with his hands, as much with his eye, the contours and textures and molding of the stone. Finally, he turned to me and said, "Men can only work this well if they want to work this well, and love the doing of it." Another time, the artist who is responsible for the ironwork said something like this: "Working on these things has been the greatest sort of experience for us. For once we have been able to do our best, with no rush, no pressure. We have been allowed to be patient." And he showed me the fruits of the patience in his work—not only the obvious beauty of it, but the hidden things, delicate details of form and texture that were there only because he had been allowed to be patient. And finally, I stood with one of the men who built the floor, just looking at it, and he said, "I love that floor. You know why? Because we made you the most beautiful floor we could."

Reverend Banse added that what struck him was

. . . the love and devotion reflected in each of these comments. What a wonderful thing it is when artisans and craftspeople are set free to make use of the gifts and talents that God has given them. In my estimation, that freedom given to them through the people of Trinity, and particularly by Mr. and Mrs. Paul Mellon, was one of the greatest blessings found and exercised in the building of this church. And so, I say, every time I walk into this place, "Thanks be to God!"

Bunny Mellon passed away on March 17, 2014. It was the end of a lifetime that had spanned over a century, and it was the end of an era. Soon afterward, the auctioneers diverged onto the properties of this twentieth-century arbiter of taste and emptied the contents of her rooms, her closets, her shelves, even what was under her bed, much of which she probably would have described as important, and some not as much—the jewelry, the furniture, the little pillows, the china, the artwork. They carried it all away—these elements of her style—to where it was all so grandly displayed on a stage set of what had been dubbed the "Auction of the Century" and sold to the highest bidders. The outcome of the auction surpassed everyone's wildest expectations as the dollars rolled in. Indeed, Bunny Mellon had spun everything she touched into gold.

How did this happen? Was it happenstance? Or was it how Bunny had spun the details of harmony, balance, scale and proportion, and the details of her life with results that had turned the design world on its head—a world that has yet to recover from the gentle manner and unassuming influence of this American icon? All because she had quietly and independently persevered and followed her own instincts—her own light. Indeed, she had come a long way from those early days of priming the pump at Grandpa Lowe's farm, garbed in her flannel nightgown. One can only imagine the pride he would have felt at the mesmerizing influence and accomplishments of his young "Bun."

Plant Medicinale by
Sophie Grandval.

AFTERWORD

BY SUSAN LEOPOLD

PAINTED LADY: THE ART OF COLLECTING BEAUTY AND KNOWLEDGE

I REMEMBER WHEN I FIRST READ ABOUT THE OAK SPRING LIBRARY AND MRS. MELLON, I was instantly enamored to find out that not far from where I lived was a woman who had a library filled with botanical treasures. I wrote to Mrs. Mellon to ask if I could come study the volumes in the collection that were written by early botanical explorers of the Blue Ridge. As a proud member of the Patawomeck tribe of Virginia and with a love for history, plants, and rare books, I wanted to write about what explorers encountered botanically in the early 1700s. My first day visiting the library to conduct research, I felt as if the landscape and whitewashed stone walls had transported me into a surreal world where the past and the present were blurred.

The library under her wing always had living plants placed throughout, such as scented geraniums and small green topiaries. Mrs. Mellon had an eye for the art of placement, be it the structure in the landscape, the layout of the orchard, or the bird bath in a courtyard; these things all felt as if they had always been there, embodying a sense of synergy and simplicity. My intuition is that Mrs. Mellon's iconic style was rooted in the art of observation and reverence for the natural order of life.

Maria Sibylla Merian (1647–1717), one of the early women artists and scientists that we know about, had this skill, apparent in the unique way in which she depicted how species were interconnected to plant life in her art. As a child, Maria was raised in a family of still-life painters. Asked to paint herbs growing in the garden, she watched observantly as caterpillars enjoyed eating the medicinal and culinary herbs. She was the first to document the transformation of caterpillars into larvae and thus their metamorphosis into butterflies. Mrs. Mellon's lifetime spanned the transformation of women breaking free from the historical cocoon of silence.

Women's role in society radically transformed during her lifetime with the right to vote and the opportunity to pursue one's passion. As a woman also passionate about plants, history, art, architecture, design, I have immense gratitude for the time that allowed me to have the experience of researching and working in the Oak Spring Library.

A great library feels like a temple to those who value its treasures, its ambience, style, and design. The Oak Spring Library is a temple tucked away on a country lane that treads across Virginia's Piedmont at the foothills on the western slopes of the Bull Run Mountains. This is where the once-great American chestnut forests thrived, but now are only present in the long-lived split-log fences that line the lanes; honoring the past in an ever-changing world, these are simple yet divine marks on the landscape that hold memory and sense of place.

Early books were culturally innovative in that they brought together uses and beliefs from a wider area than the local lore of any given region. Reading about other uses for plants, other plants that were similar but different, other species that were almost beyond imagining—this whetted the appetite for more tales from other lands.

Such books were like graphic novels of life forms from another planet, amazingly illustrated by artists and botanists who accompanied explorers, colonizers, and traders. Mrs. Mellon had a deep understanding and inquisitive nature that inspired her from a young age to collect rare botanical books before it was fashionable or valued. As biodiversity diminishes on a global scale, natural history, art, and rare books are not only extremely expensive, they are impossible to acquire. Here is the magnificent passion of one human life, and all the lives that were swept up into the quest of creative curiosity.

There is a feeling, a chorus of soft but intent presence, that arises in my memory of the Great Room of the Old Wing of the Oak Spring Garden Library from my ten-year tenure in this space. Mrs. Mellon's legacy is her style and artistry that have brought these voices and pens together in one place—manuscripts in linen boxes, countless flat drawers of prints, hand-colored etchings, botanical treasures. All bathed in the golden light of a giant Mark Rothko (1903–1979) painting that makes your heart sing. This painting is balanced by the intricate, symmetrical, stylized dandelion flower paintings of Sophie Grandval (b. 1936).

I left the Oak Spring Garden Library not long after Mrs. Mellon turned 100. I was there in her last full decade of life. In our conversations she was pensive about her mortality with her gentle comments about when she crossed over the fence, she knew her collection would live on for others to appreciate.

Her daughter, the artist Eliza Lloyd Moore (1942–2008), must have had her mother's eyes, for she wrote in 1998:

> *The more I pursue*
> *The more I see—or discover.*
> *It is more than fascinating,*
> *And through these spirits,*
> *Whether in field or studio,*
> *I am always seeing*
> *And never alone.*

Never alone in seeing, surrounded by the spirits of discovery, here is the magnificent passion of one human life, and all the lives that were swept up into the quest. All these were people of knowledge, sharing their fondest projects, their fingerprints, their breath, their curiosity, their passions, their gatherings and gleanings, their harvest, their very best work. And each of these is a compilation of the knowledge of others, hand-me-downs, generations of plant-loving, plant-knowing, plant-using farmers, healers, tribes, mothers, those who informed the explorers and the taxonomists. Their breath and fingerprints fill this grand stone treasure chest that is this library. It is the vision of one woman who was blessed with extraordinary style and the resources to gather in one place the very best of our world's botanical records and art forms.

Mrs. Mellon was authentic in her style, she intentionally treasured and valued "weeds" as much as she did the rare blue Himalayan poppy, *Meconopsis* spp. I was always amazed at the abundance of the painted lady butterflies, *Vanessa cardui* (Linnaeus, 1758), that fluttered throughout the summer in the perfectly pruned Hardy Orange orchard seen from outside the library's large, picturesque windows. The painted lady caterpillars are known to survive off more than a hundred host plants such as the thistles (*Asteraceae*), hollyhocks and mallow (*Malvaceae*), and various legumes (*Fabaceae*), perhaps symbolic of the many different botanical interests that Mrs. Mellon's life's work and her collection represented.

Mrs. Mellon's spirit embodies the painted lady, for she treasured the wildness of weeds and their ability to endure without the human hand, as well as the artful form and human interaction of a well-pruned apple tree. Our human relationship to nature is embodied in our relationship with plants. Her legacy is she left us a library and landscape to continue the exploration of this relationship. The painted lady butterflies capture Mrs. Mellon's spirit as a patron to the arts as well as a library founded by a woman whose iconic style is a true American treasure.

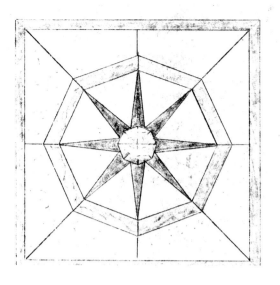
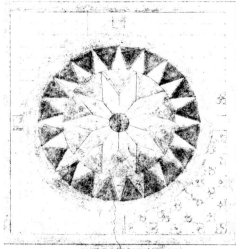

Two block patterns, both presumably for floors. Compass sketch on the left is seen in Nantucket, page 203.

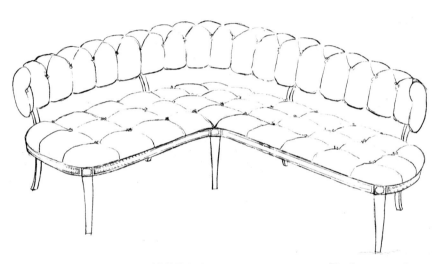

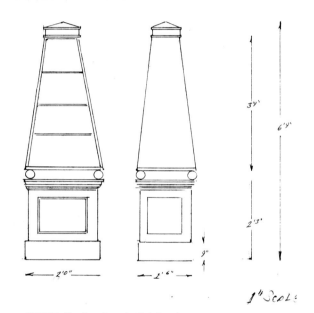

ABOVE AND BELOW LEFT AND RIGHT: The banquette in New York, seen on page 155. Drawings not to scale, Leonard noted.

ABOVE: Design for obelisk bookcase.

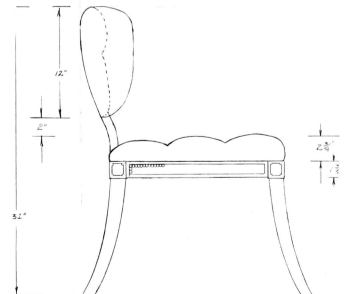

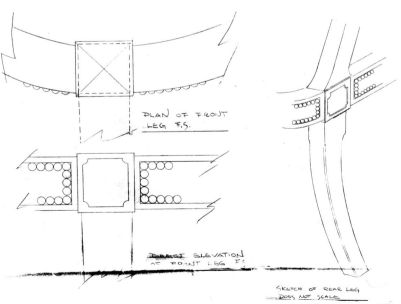

PAUL LEONARD, DESIGN COLLABORATOR

Paul Leonard was a patient genius whose creative designs infused a mix of authenticity and honeycomb sweetness into Bunny's décor. For more than ten years, Leonard executed the artistic effects, in collaboration with Bunny, at all of her houses. His artistry included the painted floor designs throughout her homes. Here are some of his sketches for floors, furniture, and a lighting fixture.

SUSPENDED ELECTRIC CANDELABRA
FOR MELLON HOUSE 125 E 70TH ST NYC.
TO BE CONSTRUCTED OF BRASS. ANTIQUED
TO MATCH EXISTING LANTERN.
SCALE - FULL SIZE.   4-28-67

Top of candelabra.

PHOTOGRAPHIC CREDITS

Cristóbal Balenciaga Museum, courtesy: 278, 281–3

John Baskett, courtesy: 135TR, 176TL, 178TR, 180BR

Jonathan Becker: 97

Tory Burch, courtesy: 221, 222

Bee Dabney, courtesy: 36B

Patrick Demarchelier, courtesy: 9

Fitchburg Historical Society, courtesy: 42–3

Kathy and David Fleming, courtesy: 27, 39

Joshua Greene © 2021: 105, 287

Collection of the Historical Society of Princeton, published in MS938.3.1: 28T, 28B, 31, 32T, 32B

Linda Jane Holden, © 2021: 83L, 83R

Bryan Huffman, © 2021: 35TL, 35BL, 35BR, 36TL, 36TM, 36TR, 37, 47, 54T, 58M, 77TR, 82MM, 84L, 88L, 89T, 94R, 99L, 106, 107, 121BL, 121BR, 122, 124BL, 124BM, 124BR, 129TL, 129TM, 164, 167BL, 168TL, 178TR, 183R, 182TL, 182TR, 183, 188, 189TL, 189TR, 189MR, 189BL, 190, 191, 192, 194

John F. Kennedy Presidential Library and Museum, Boston, photographer Abbie Rowe, White House Photographs, courtesy: 17L, 17R

Schuyler Knapp, courtesy: 127, 128, 129TR, 129ML, 129MR, 129BL, 129BR

Desiree Lee, courtesy: 100, 101, 124TR, 124MR

Paul Leonard, courtesy Samantha Leonard: 61B, 92, 154B, 157, 181TR, 189BR, 296–7

Susan Leopold, courtesy: 292

Thomas Lloyd, © 2021: 15, 19TL, 19ML, 19BL, 23L, 23M, 23R, 35TR, 41, 46, 53, 54B, 57T, 60, 61T, 75T, 77B, 79BL, 79BR, 84R, 85, 88TR, 89BL, 90T, 91, 92L, 95B, 103T, 104BL, 104BR, 108, 109, 111T, 111B, 134, 135RL, 135BL, 135BR, 136–139, 147, 158B, 163T, 167T, 167BR, 168TR, 167BL, 178TL, 178B, 180BL, 181TL, 181MR, 181BR, 182B, 184TL, 184TR, 184B, 185, 195T, 195BR, 203BR, 209T, 109B, 228TL, 232TL, 232TR, 232BR, 233 all, 238, 239, 242–55, 257R, 258–63, 280, 288TR

Cathy Mellon, courtesy: 5

National Gallery of Art, Washington, courtesy: pp. 72, 73, 146

National Gallery of Art, Washington, DC, Gallery Archives, courtesy. 26B, National Gallery of Art Event Images: p. 19R—Photograph by Jim Sugar, 26B4_22284_006; p. 20 top to bottom, left to right—26B4_304_021, 26B_304_023, 26B4_304_026, 26B4_304_027, 26B4_304_024, 26B4_304_033; p. 21 above and below left—26B4_304_005, 26B4_304_002; p. 21 below right—National Gallery of Art, Washington, DC, Gallery Archives. 26B, National Gallery of Art Event Images. Photograph by Jim Sugar, 26B4_456_001

Collection of Oak Spring Garden Foundation, Upperville, VA: 63, 67T, 90B, 92R, 95T, 96T, 98BR, 102, 171BR, 175, 176BL, 177, 179, 180T, 182, 186, 187, 210, 211T, 224T, 232BL, 234, 284, 286R, 288TL, 288BL, 288BR, 289 all

> Watercolors by Snowy Campbell: 62, 69, 77TL, 130, 132, 133, 140, 141, 142, 149, 153BR, 156, 158T, 159,

> Michael Dunne, photographer: 55T, 55B, 57B, 58L, 59, 66, 67B, 68, 74T, 76BL,78–80, 81T, 82BR, 88B, 89BR, 93, 98TL, 98TR, 98BL, 99R, 103B, 112–13, 114, 116, 117, 119, 120, 121T, 123, 145R, 150–1, 153T, 153BL, 154T, 155, 160–1, 163B, 168BR, 170, 171T, 172–3, 174, 211B, 212–13, 214, 215, 220, 224B, 225, 226L, 226R, 227R, 228TR, 228B, 229, 230, 231

> Joshua Greene, photographer: 287

> Watercolors by Mossy Fuller: 206, 227L

> Mark Peebler, photographer: 104T

> Watercolors by Isabelle Rey: 234, 236–7, 240–1, 256–7

Sotheby's Inc., courtesy of, © 2021: 2, 6, 50, 64–5, 70, 71, 74BL, 74BR, 75BL, 75BR, 76TL, 76TM, 76TR, 76ML, 76MR, 76BR, 82TM, 82TR, 82ML, 82MR, 82BL, 86, 87, 94L, 115, 144, 276TL, 276TM, 276TR, 276MR, 277BL, 277BR

Draza Stamenich, courtesy: 96B, 124TL, 195BL

Daniel Sutherland: 195BM, 197–202, 203TL 203TR, 203BL, 204–5, 216, 219, 223

Courtesy Philippe Venet, courtesy: 286L

Virginia Museum of Fine Arts, Richmond, courtesy, as follows:

p. 266:
Jean Schlumberger, designer (French, 1907–1987), Tiffany & Company, manufacturer (American, founded 1853)
Dot Losange Bangles, designed 1960, made late 20th century
18-karat gold, paillonné enamel
Virginia Museum of Fine Arts, Richmond.
Collection of Mr. Paul Mellon
Photo: Travis Fullerton, © Virginia Museum of Fine Arts, © Virginia Museum of Fine Arts

p. 268:
Jean Schlumberger (French, 1907–1987)
Shells, 1958
Platinum, 18-karat gold, diamond, sapphire and emerald
1 ⅝"W × 7 ⅛"L
4.13 cm × 18.1 cm
Marks: *Tiffany Schlumberger; IRID PLAT 18k*
Virginia Museum of Fine Arts, Richmond.
Collection of Mrs. Paul Mellon
Photo: Travis Fullerton, © Virginia Museum of Fine Arts, © Virginia Museum of Fine Arts

p. 269:
Jean Schlumberger, designer (French, 1907–1987), Tiffany & Company, manufacturer (American, founded 1853)
Butterflies, 1956
Amethyst, sapphires, turquoise, peridots, yellow diamonds, diamonds, colored stones, 18-karat gold, platinum
1 ½"W × 7"L
3.81 cm × 17.78 cm
Marks: signed *Tiffany Schlumberger, 18k*
Virginia Museum of Fine Arts, Richmond. Collection of Mrs. Paul Mellon
Photo: Travis Fullerton, ⓒ Virginia Museum of Fine Arts, ⓒ Virginia Museum of Fine Arts

p. 270TL:
Jean Schlumberger (French, 1907–1987)
Study for 'Flower Pot': Flower, ca. 1960
graphite on tracing paper
6"H × 4 ½ "W
15.24 cm × 11.4 cm
Virginia Museum of Fine Arts, Richmond. Gift of the Estate of Jean Schlumberger
Photo: Troy Wilkinson, ⓒ Virginia Museum of Fine Arts, ⓒ Virginia Museum of Fine Arts

p. 270BL:
Jean Schlumberger (French, 1907–1987)
Study for "Flower Pot": Pot Designs, ca. 1960
Graphite on tracing paper
11 ¹⁵/₁₆ "H × 8 ¹⁵/₁₆"W
30.32 cm × 22.7 cm
Virginia Museum of Fine Arts, Richmond. Gift of the Estate of Jean Schlumberger
Photo: Troy Wilkinson, ⓒ Virginia Museum of Fine Arts, ⓒ Virginia Museum of Fine Arts

p. 270TR:
Jean Schlumberger (French, 1907–1987)
Flower Pot (Pot de fleurs), 1960
Amethyst, emeralds, diamonds, black garnet ore, 18, 20, and 22 carat gold, terracotta
7 ¼"H × 4"W × 4"D
18.42 cm × 10.16 cm × 10.16 cm
Marks: stamped on bottom, *Tiffany - Schlumberger*
Virginia Museum of Fine Arts, Richmond. Collection of Mrs. Paul Mellon
Photo: Travis Fullerton, ⓒ Virginia Museum of Fine Arts, ⓒ Virginia Museum of Fine Arts

pp. 270BR and 271BL:
Jean Schlumberger, designer (French, 1907–1987), Tiffany & Company, manufacturer (American, founded 1853)
Dahlia Hidden-Watch, 1958
18 karat gold, diamonds and citrines
6 ⁷/₁₆"L × 1 ¼"W × ½"D
16.35 cm × 3.18 cm × 1.27 cm
Marks: signed *Tiffany Schlumberger, 18k*
Virginia Museum of Fine Arts, Richmond. Collection of Mrs. Paul Mellon
Photo: Travis Fullerton, ⓒ Virginia Museum of Fine Arts, ⓒ Virginia Museum of Fine Arts

p. 271R:
Jean Schlumberger (French, 1907–1987, active in the United States)
Table Clock, ca. 1962
Lapis lazuli, gold
9 ½"H × 5 ⅛"W × 5 ⅛"D
24.13 cm × 13.02 cm × 13.02 cm
Marks: stamped on bottom, *SCHLUMBERGER/ PARIS*
Virginia Museum of Fine Arts, Richmond. Collection of Mrs. Paul Mellon
Photo: Katherine Wetzel, ⓒ Virginia Museum of Fine Arts, ⓒ Virginia Museum of Fine Arts

p. 272:
Jean Schlumberger, designer (French, 1907–1987), Tiffany & Co., manufacturer (American, founded 1837)
Jasmine
18 karat gold, platinum, colored sapphire and diamond
1 ¾"W × 19"L
4.45 cm × 48.26 cm
Marks: signed *Tiffany Schlumberger, Made in France*
Virginia Museum of Fine Arts, Richmond. Collection of Mrs. Paul Mellon
Photo: Travis Fullerton, ⓒ Virginia Museum of Fine Arts, ⓒ Virginia Museum of Fine Arts

p. 273TL:
Jean Schlumberger, (French, 1907–1987), Tiffany and Company, manufacturer (American, founded 1837)
Leaves (Necklace), 1956
Platinum, 18 karat gold, turquoise, diamonds
1 ½"W × 14"L (3.81 cm × 35.56 cm)
Signed *Tiffany & Co. Schlumberger*
Marks: *IRID.PLAT*
Virginia Museum of Fine Arts, Richmond. Collection of Mrs. Paul Mellon
Photo: Travis Fullerton, ⓒ Virginia Museum of Fine Arts, ⓒ Virginia Museum of Fine Arts

p. 273TR:
Jean Schlumberger (French, 1907–1987), Tiffany and Company, manufacturer (American, founded 1853)
Flowers and Leaves, ca. 1958
18-karat gold, platinum and diamonds
1 ¼"W × 13 ¼"L (3.18 × 33.6 cm)
Signed *Tiffany Schlumberger*
Marks: *Made in France*
Virginia Museum of Fine Arts, Richmond. Collection of Mrs. Paul Mellon
Photo: Travis Fullerton, ⓒ Virginia Museum of Fine Arts, ⓒ Virginia Museum of Fine Arts

p. 273ML&BL:
Jean Schlumberger (French, 1907–1987)
Torsades, ca. 1958
18-karat gold, diamonds, gold beads and coral beads
1a: Coral Bracelet without clasp:
8 ⅝"L × ⅝"W × ½"D (1.91 × 1.59 × 1.27 cm)
1b-c: Gold Bracelet with diamond clasp:
8 ⅛"L × ¾"W × 1 ¹/₁₆"D (20.64 × 1.91 × 1.75 cm)
Virginia Museum of Fine Arts, Richmond. Collection of Mrs. Paul Mellon
Photo: Travis Fullerton, ⓒ Virginia Museum of Fine Arts, ⓒ Virginia Museum of Fine Arts

p. 273BR:
Jean Schlumberger, designer (French, 1907–1987), Tiffany & Company, manufacturer (American, founded 1853)
Necklace, late 1950s
Cultured pearl, fancy colored diamond and sapphires
Overall (with clasp): 15 in. (38.1 cm)
Marks: signed *Tiffany Schlumberger*
Virginia Museum of Fine Arts, Richmond. Collection of Mrs. Paul Mellon
Photo: Travis Fullerton, ⓒ Virginia Museum of Fine Arts, ⓒ Virginia Museum of Fine Arts

p. 274:
Jean Schlumberger, designer (French, 1907–1987), Tiffany & Company, manufacturer (American, founded 1853)
Flower with Detachable Leaf, 1964 18 karat gold, platinum, diamonds and sapphires
2 ½"H × 1 ¾"W × 1 ½"D
6.35 cm × 4.45 cm × 3.81 cm
Marks: signed *Tiffany Schlumberger*, numbered *741*
Virginia Museum of Fine Arts, Richmond. Collection of Mrs. Paul Mellon
Photo: Travis Fullerton, ⓒ Virginia Museum of Fine Arts, ⓒ Virginia Museum of Fine Arts

Virginia Museum of Fine Arts, Richmond (continued)

p. 275TL:
Jean Schlumberger, designer (French, 1907–1987), Tiffany & Company, manufacturer (American, founded 1853)
Cruciform Pendant, early 1970s
18 karat gold, platinum, rubies and diamond
1 5/8"H × 1 3/8"W × 1/4"D
4.13 cm × 3.49 cm × 0.64 cm
Marks: signed *Tiffany & Co. Schlumberger*, numbered *750* and *PT850*
Virginia Museum of Fine Arts, Richmond.
Collection of Mrs. Paul Mellon
Photo: Travis Fullerton, © Virginia Museum of Fine Arts, © Virginia Museum of Fine Arts

p. 275TR:
Jean Schlumberger (French, 1907–1987)
Ear Clips, 1960s
18-karat gold, lapis lazuli, diamonds, cultured pearls
1 3/16"H × 3/4"W × 5/8"D
3.02 cm × 1.91 cm × 1.59 cm
Marks: .1 signed *Schlumberger*, both have illegible marks
Virginia Museum of Fine Arts, Richmond.
Collection of Mrs. Paul Mellon
Photo: Travis Fullerton, © Virginia Museum of Fine Arts, © Virginia Museum of Fine Arts

p. 275BL: Jean Schlumberger, designer (French, 1907–1987), Tiffany & Company, manufacturer (American, founded 1853)
Sea Star, 1960
Platinum, 18 karat gold, rubies and diamonds
2 1/4"H × 2 1/4"W × 5/8"D
5.72 cm × 5.72 cm × 1.59 cm
Marks: signed *Tiffany Schlumberger, Made in France*
Virginia Museum of Fine Arts, Richmond.
Collection of Mrs. Paul Mellon
Photo: Travis Fullerton, © Virginia Museum of Fine Arts, © Virginia Museum of Fine Arts

p. 275BR:
Jean Schlumberger, designer (French, 1907–1987), Tiffany & Company, manufacturer (American, founded 1853)
Bleuet, ca. 1957
Sapphires, diamonds, 18-karat gold, platinum
1 7/8"H × 1 7/8"W × 5/8"D
4.76 cm × 4.76 cm × 1.59 cm
Marks: signed *Tiffany Schlumberger, Made in France*
Virginia Museum of Fine Arts, Richmond.
Collection of Mrs. Paul Mellon
Photo: Travis Fullerton, © Virginia Museum of Fine Arts, © Virginia Museum of Fine Arts

p. 276ML:
Jean Schlumberger (French, 1907–1987)
Salt Cellar, 1965
Enamel and 18 carat gold
2 3/4"H × 2 1/2"Dia.
6.99 cm × 6.35 cm
Marks: marked on bottom: *Schlumberger Paris*
Virginia Museum of Fine Arts, Richmond.
Collection of Mrs. Paul Mellon
Photo: Katherine Wetzel, © Virginia Museum of Fine Arts, © Virginia Museum of Fine Arts

p. 276MM:
Jean Schlumberger (French, 1907–1987)
Salt Cellar, 1965
Enamel and 18 carat gold
2 3/4"H × 2 1/2"Dia.
6.99 cm × 6.35 cm
Marks: marked on bottom: *Schlumberger Paris*
Virginia Museum of Fine Arts, Richmond.
Collection of Mrs. Paul Mellon
Photo: Katherine Wetzel, © Virginia Museum of Fine Arts, © Virginia Museum of Fine Arts

p. 276BL cluster:
Jean Schlumberger, designer (French, 1907–1987), Tiffany & Company, manufacturer (American, founded 1853)
Banana Clips, after 1967
18-karat gold and paillonné enamel
Virginia Museum of Fine Arts, Richmond.
Collection of Mrs. Paul Mellon
Photo: Travis Fullerton, © Virginia Museum of Fine Arts, © Virginia Museum of Fine Arts

p. 277TL:
Jean Schlumberger, designer (French, 1907–1987), Tiffany & Company, manufacturer (American, founded 1853)
Basket-Weave Case with Flowers, ca. 1965
Diamonds, enamel and 18 karat two-color gold
3 1/4"H × 3 1/2"W × 1 7/8"D
8.26 cm × 8.89 cm × 4.76 cm
Marks: signed *Tiffany & Co. Schlumberger, France, 18k*, numbered *5549, 489*
Virginia Museum of Fine Arts, Richmond.
Collection of Mrs. Paul Mellon
Photo: Travis Fullerton, © Virginia Museum of Fine Arts, © Virginia Museum of Fine Arts

p. 277TR:
Jean Schlumberger, designer (French, 1907–1987), Tiffany & Company, manufacturer (American, founded 1853)
Basket-Weave Case, 1959, model 1956
Sapphire, 18-karat gold
1 3/8"H × 1 3/4"W × 4 3/8"L
3.49 cm × 4.45 cm × 11.11 cm
Virginia Museum of Fine Arts, Richmond.
Collection of Mrs. Paul Mellon
Photo: Travis Fullerton, © Virginia Museum of Fine Arts, © Virginia Museum of Fine Arts

West Rindge Historical Society, courtesy: 44–5